PROFESSIONAL NURSE SERIES

Supervision in Nursing Practice

WITHDRAWN

PROFESSIONAL NURSE SERIES

Supervision in Nursing Practice

K Jooste

JUTA

Supervision in Nursing Practice

© Juta and Co Ltd, 2009
PO Box 24309
Lansdowne 7779
Cape Town, South Africa

Disclaimer
In the writing of this book, every effort has been made to present accurate and up-to-date information from the best and most reliable sources. However, the results of nursing individuals depend on a variety of factors that are beyond the control of the authors and publishers. Therefore, neither the authors nor the publishers assume responsibility for, nor make any warranty as regards to, the outcomes achieved from the procedures described in this book.

ISBN 978 07021 8051 4

Project management: Johanna Breakey
Proofreading and editing: Ethné Clarke
Indexer: Ethné Clarke
Cover design: Genevieve Simpson
Typeset in Berkeley Oldstyle Book 11 pt on 13 pt by Charlene Bate
Print Management by Print Communications

Contents

List of books available in this series

Professional Nurse Series: *Acute Care*
- *Clinical Assessment and Treatment of Acutely Ill Patients*

Professional Nurse Series: *Infection Control Made Easy*
- *A Hospital Guide for Health Professionals*

Professional Nurse Series: *Palliative Care*

Professional Nurse Series: *The Partograph and How to Assess Labour*

Professional Nurse Series: *Record Keeping*

Professional Nurse Series: *Supervision in Nursing Practice*

Forthcoming Title
Professional Nurse Series: *Forensics for Nurses*

How to use this book

This publication forms part of a series for the continuous professional development of professional nurses. The overall goal of this series is to provide an integrated approach to the topic under discussion. Each book in the series can be used by individuals or groups or as an education and training resource by nursing education institutions for learning experiences on the topic addressed.

An author who has knowledge and expertise in the particular subject has prepared each publication. It is hoped that this book will meet your learning and development needs by presenting the content in an easily accessible and user-friendly way that will facilitate learning.

Each publication addresses a specific topic in nursing, and is divided into separate chapters. The introduction includes:
- learning outcomes that you could expect to achieve after completing the course,
- the learning that is assumed to be in place, and
- key ethical and legislative considerations of which the nurse should take cognisance.

Each chapter contains:
- information and examples relating to the topic,
- learning activities with questions that allow you to apply the information in your own context,
- case study(ies) relating to the content of the chapter, and
- notes containing tips and precautions for your information, where applicable.

A separate answer guide, containing main points for consideration, is included on page 53 of this book.

Enjoy the learning experience!

Nelouise Geyer
Series editor

Introduction

Supervision is an activity that all nurse supervisors in all health-care organisations carry out. Nurse supervisors are placed in clinics and hospitals to supervise student nurses as they complete the practical requirements of their training programmes. Even at primary health-care level we want to strengthen supervision in clinics so that the quality of care improves (Speech by the Minister of Health, 2006).

Research has shown that supervisors who have received specific training are more effective than those who have not received specific training. Some formal training is necessary for engaging in the supervision process and one of the most accessible methods is through continuous training (O'Connor, 2008:14).

For individuals to develop the knowledge and skills to become effective supervisors they must first go through the process of effective supervision themselves – particularly in terms of being supervised and mentored in the role of supervision.

The term 'supervisor' typically refers to one's immediate superior in the workplace, that is, the person to whom you report directly in the organisation. For example, a middle manager's supervisor typically would be a top manager. A first-line manager's supervisor would be a middle manager. A worker's supervisor typically would be a first-line manager.

'Supervision' means different things at different stages of our development as practitioners and the amount of supervision required in a clinical setting will also vary. Supervision is a very personal matter and unless supervisors attend formal training, supervision provided by them is likely to be based on their experience rather than based on sound principles. Supervision is the activity carried out by supervisors to oversee the performance or productivity and progress of their supervisees, who report directly to them.

Learning outcomes

Supervisors should have the appropriate knowledge, skills, values and attitudes that enable them to monitor the performance of supervisees within the professional, legal and ethical framework of nursing practice. As a supervisor, you should identify solutions to problems, improve the standards of patient care, further develop your skills and knowledge, and improve the understanding of your own practice.

Specific outcomes

On completion of this course you should be able to:

- Explain the different roles, skills and styles of an effective supervisor
- Interpret scenarios in which supervision should be effectively implemented
- Distinguish between the types of supervision in practice
- Describe the purpose of supervision in your own working environment
- Evaluate your own supervisory performance to be able to improve your role in the unit
- Evaluate your unit according to set standards, to determine the extent to which supervision is needed in your unit
- Monitor your unit setting to prevent medico-legal hazards and negligence to patients.

Learning assumed to be in place

The supervisor should have a basic knowledge of the following:

- Unit management, with specific reference to the management process (planning, organising, directing and control) of financial and human resources in nursing practice
- Her/his role as a team member, communicator and coordinator of staff in a group where dynamics and conflict management exist.

Key ethical considerations

The most important **ethical principles** to be followed in supervision are:

- Accuracy of findings
- The safety of the patient/client
- Advocacy for the rights of individuals, families, groups and communities
- Respect for the uniqueness of each staff member and client.

Key legal and professional considerations

Nurse supervisors need to act as role models for supervisees and demonstrate accountability for their actions by:

● Practising within their scope of practice

● Continuously monitoring the competencies of supervisees, to support and promote staff development of supervisees

● Respecting the rights of patients/clients and supervisees.

Key terms used in this course

Supervision: A process that consists of a variety of patterns of behaviour, the appropriateness of which depends on the needs, competencies, expectations and philosophies of the supervisor and supervisee and the specifics of the situation (task, client, setting). It aims at the growth and development of the supervisor and supervisee to result in optimal service to the client (O'Connor, 2008:14).

Supervisor: A supervisor is in charge of a nursing section or unit. Supervisors should only supervise in those areas of nursing practice where they are competent. In other speciality areas they should arrange for supervision by an appropriately trained colleague. Supervisors should have competence not only in the areas of clinical practice they will supervise, but in the theory and techniques of supervision itself. Having once been a supervisee oneself is not an adequate credential for providing clinical supervision.

Supervisee: A professional nurse or student nurse who has certain training and competence needs. The supervisor should determine the nature and extent of additional training and supervision needed. This should be reassessed over the course of supervision and responded to accordingly. Generic supervision is inadequate, because supervision should be responsive to the particular training needs of a supervisee. Other terms used interchangeably for supervisee are staff member or team member.

Nursing unit: Any clinical nursing environment in which a supervisor is allocated to a supervisee.

CHAPTER ONE

The conceptualisation of supervision

Key concepts

A supervisor engages in:

- **The act** of overseeing supervisees or watching over the work or tasks of another who may lack full knowledge of the responsibility at hand. This entails being in charge of a group of people engaged in an activity or task and keeping order or ensuring that they perform it correctly.

- **The process** or occupation of supervising. This involves direction and inspection, which does not mean control of another but guidance in a work or professional context.

- **Critical evaluation** which means to oversee and to have oversight of super-intendence.

These concepts lead to various conceptual definitions of nurse supervision. Here are two examples:
- Supervision is a formal process of professional support and learning, undertaken through a range of activities, which enables individual professional nurses to develop knowledge and competence, assume responsibility for their own practice and enhance service-user protection, quality and safety of care in complex clinical situations.
- Supervision is central to the process of learning and to the expansion of the scope of practice, and should be seen as a means of encouraging self-assessment and analytical and reflective skills.

Supervision therefore often includes:
- Conducting basic management skills (decision-making, problem-solving, planning and delegation)
- Organising teams
- Noticing the need for and designing new job roles in the group
- Being involved in hiring new nursing staff
- Training new supervisees
- Undertaking supervisee performance management (setting goals, observing and giving feedback, addressing performance issues, disciplinary procedures, etc.)
- Ensuring conformance to staff policies and other internal regulations.

Nurse supervisors should continuously remind themselves about the reasons for acting as supervisor. They could therefore create a bookmark as in Figure 1.1, to remind themselves of the importance of their role.

BOOKMARK

Top 10 reasons for supervising a student nurse:
1   Develop and retain the new student nurse
2   Stay up to date
3   Share your expertise with the student nurse
4   Promote interpersonal relationships in the unit
5   Act as an advocate for quality services to be rendered
6   Foster an effective multi-disciplinary team spirit
7   Promote the image of nursing
8   Develop own supervisory skills
9   Enhance clinical skills through the teaching function
10   Act as a role model.

Figure1.1   Bookmark of reasons for supervising a student nurse

Learning activity 1
Bookmark on supervision

Complete the bookmark on page 33.

Indicate the top 10 reasons why a nursing student should be supervised. This bookmark will remind you why you should act as a nurse supervisor for students undergoing training.

PURPOSE OF SUPERVISION

It is important that the appropriate purpose for supervision is clearly established.

The purpose of supervision is to:
● provide support, guidance and development opportunities
● observe and receive information from qualified sources
● provide direct, constructive feedback about professional practice
● identify professional behaviour and practices that should be recognised as exemplars
● identify professional behaviours and practices that may require an evaluation
● support service delivery improvement and staff development.

Ten overall purposes of supervision can be considered:
1. Professional learning and development, and teaching the supervisee in order to facilitate the supervisee's professional and personal development
2. Providing a forum to assess the nurse–patient relationship
3. Protecting the welfare and best interest of the client by promoting accountable health-care services and programmes and accepting shared responsibility for client care
4. Lending support to staff members who are team members in the multidisciplinary team, to enable them to manage the often intense nature of the work and replenish the emotional resources needed to maintain professionalism
5. Providing the supervisee with a safe, protective relationship in which to be creative and to develop knowledge, understanding and skills; to provide positive stimulation and safety for the supervisee; to promote excellence within an ethical and safe practice; to provide developmental support to the supervisee; to provide an opportunity for evaluation of the practice; to enable the supervisee to maintain ethical and professional standards of practice and to ensure accountability to keep practitioners safe
6. Monitoring the supervisee's performance and development by addressing and re-mediating problems in a timely fashion; serving as gatekeeper to the profession; providing monitoring of professional practice of supervisees and monitoring levels and priorities of workload
7. Empowering the trainee to self-supervise as an independent professional
8. Improving own supervisory skills by improving instruction skills and capabilities; providing opportunities to develop decision-making skills and explore new possibilities, furnishing ways to reflect on and work through problems; affording chances to develop a personal theory and promoting competencies in acting as a counsellor
9. Providing an opportunity to raise issues arising from practice; to reflect upon practice, consider strategies and solutions to different problems and to develop professionalism within by taking on the role of a personal adviser
10. Ensuring quality assurance in service delivery as supervision can offer a mechanism for quality assurance to ensure effective and consistent service delivery.

Learning activity 2
Scenario

Professional nurse A is appointed in a medical unit of an academic training hospital, after working in a paediatric unit for five years. After two weeks she is appointed as sister in charge of the 30-bed unit. A bedridden HIV/Aids patient, Mr X, is admitted to the unit in the left wing, and after two days starts complaining that nurses do not treat his back and pressure parts regularly. Student nurses delivering nursing care for Mr X explain that he is just a difficult patient. A week later a bedsore is noted by a first-year student nurse but not reported or recorded. Two days later a third-year student nurse reports sepsis of the bedsore to professional nurse B who initiates a back and pressure part nursing record, for the patient to be turned every two hours. Three days later the patient develops a high fever and the doctor is informed about the bedsore and fever of the patient. On the doctor's round the medical practitioner makes a diagnosis that the patient has systemic sepsis. The patient dies a week later after receiving all prescribed medical treatment. The family of Mr X writes a complaint to the hospital and the South African Nursing Council (SANC) and accuses the nursing staff of negligence in delivering adequate nursing care. On investigation it becomes apparent that on some days only student nurses were allocated to the left wing where the patient was treated.

The sister in charge of the unit is also summoned by the SANC to appear before a disciplinary committee with the charge of negligence in supervision of Mr X's care.

When reflecting on this scenario, it can be seen that the sister in charge had certain responsibilities as a supervisor. Which purposes of supervision were neglected? Complete Activity 2 on pages 33–35.

THE LEGAL, PROFESSIONAL, ETHICAL AND CULTURAL FRAMEWORK WITHIN WHICH SUPERVISION TAKES PLACE

Role players in supervision have certain rights and responsibilities. These are given below.

Legal framework

The supervisor and supervisee should act within their own scope of practice as stipulated by the Nursing Act No 33 of 2005.

Regarding legal matters on supervision, consult with an attorney before taking or recommending action(s). If the role players are dissatisfied with how the supervisory process or the relationship is proceeding, try discussing this, but if this is not productive you should consult a human resources adviser.

Professional responsibilities

Accurate representation of your qualifications and competencies is essential. Be sure you represent and advertise yourself in a manner that does not imply competence or licence that you do not have. Make sure your patients know you are receiving supervision. A clear identification tag should be worn.

Ethical considerations

Supervisors should utilise a comprehensive *informed consent* process at the beginning of the supervisory relationship. Be sure it includes meeting time and location, how to reach the supervisor between supervisory sessions, emergency arrangements, the nature and timing or evaluative procedures to be used and with whom they will be shared, and an agreement on all responsibilities for each individual. The expectations of both the supervisor and the supervisee should be clear. This agreement should be updated to include any changes that may occur during the course of supervision.
The supervisory process should feel *safe*, not threatening or punitive. It should provide a forum for guided learning that offers enough security and safety so that you will not be afraid to try anything new, or fear failure. If this safe environment does not develop, a discussion will be needed between the role players or a trusted adviser.

A *trusting* relationship should exist between role players. Supervisors hold more power than supervisees in the supervisory relationship and should not take advantage of the trust in or dependence on them. All their actions and behaviours should be consistent with the goals of the training and professional development needs of the supervisee. Ensure that both the level and intensity of supervision are adequate for the needs of the supervisee. Remember that if a staff member is unlicensed, the supervisor is responsible for all he/she does professionally. All treatment notes should be reviewed. A supervisor should not merely ask how things are going with the patients.

Ensure that informed consent agreements of patients address the limits of *confidentiality* to include the supervisor's involvement in the treatment process. Patients have the right to know what information will be shared with the supervisor and how this information will be utilised.

In addition to thorough documentation of clinical services provided, both the supervisee and the supervisor should keep a record on a supervisory document during the supervisory sessions to include any recommendations made by them to follow up with patients. Maintain this *supervisory record* as one would with other clinical records. This will help ensure greater accountability and resolve any differences about what transpired during supervision. Review notes of supervisory sessions over time to check for trends and patterns that may be important to discuss later.

Supervisors should expect supervisees to be knowledgeable of their *ethical codes of conduct* and *pledge of service*.

Cultural diversity

Supervisors should be sensitive to diversity issues between themselves and the supervisees, as well as with regard to each patient's treatment. Issues to consider include age, race, ethnicity, culture, gender, religion and sexual orientation. These issues should be addressed in a manner that does not feel threatening or make you feel uncomfortable. The Constitution of the country should be abided by.

Supervisory contract

Arrangements for supervision should be agreed to between supervisors and supervisees, and formalised in either a verbal or written contract. When negotiating such a contract, certain aspects should be taken into account such as:
- Job descriptions
- Policies and priorities
- Supervisor's expectations
- Supervisee's expectations
- Team expectations
- The focus and content of the contract
- The method of supervision
- Any arrangements that need to be made to fulfil the contract.

Learning activity 3

Supervisory contract

Draw up a supervisory contract document in which you describe your legal, professional, ethical and cultural roles and responsibilities within which supervision with a supervisee will take place. Use the framework provided on page 35.

Tips for nurses

Supervisors:

- Watch over the work or tasks of a supervisee who may lack full knowledge of a responsibility to be carried out.
- Keep order in the daily activities of followers.
- Monitor if tasks were performed correctly.
- Guide supervisees who ask questions on issues that they are unsure about, in a professional manner.
- Evaluate critically if you are fulfilling your purpose as a supervisor.
- Assume responsibility for your own practice.
- Focus on quality nursing care and the safety of the patient.

Student nurses:

- Remember the serious professional obligation you have to your patients, to your supervisor, and to the profession.
- Take your training seriously and keep in mind the great impact you have on your patients' lives.
- Utilise your supervisor as a professional role model.

Precautions

- Do not believe what you cannot see or read!
- Ask if you do not know.
- If you are a supervisee and feel that the supervisory experience is not adequately meeting your training needs, be proactive and assertive. It is **your** professional training.

METHODS OF SUPERVISION

There are several ways that supervision sessions can be organised, as discussed below.

Peer supervision is either on a one-to-one basis or within a small group setting. The obvious advantage is that the universal identification provided by peer supervision provides a sound platform from which to launch supervised sessions. The team leader or manager's role in peer supervision is purely as a monitoring exercise and he/she is not part of the actual supervision process. Peer supervision may have a tendency to overemphasise support. Peers may collude in not challenging one another, and may have little to offer in terms of skills development and in ensuring clinical standards are met.

In *team supervision*, the focus is on the team objectives as opposed to individual work. It is usually facilitated by one identified supervisor. Possibilities for team/group supervision should be explained with reference to common identified needs, effective application of resources and the dynamics of peer learning. The application of group learning should be appropriate to the group, context and needs.

Records of supervisory discussions should be accurate, up to date, and available to guide development and further *consultative supervision*.

Shadow supervision is where one nurse, possibly a student or a newly appointed nurse undertaking an induction programme, is attached as a shadow to an experienced nurse, to learn by observation.

Managerial or tutorial supervision is the process in which the team leader supervises an individual nurse formally and privately.

Two other forms of supervision are *pair and live supervision*. Pair supervision involves two nurses being supervised by their team leader or manager. Live supervision can also be carried out during the actual nurse–patient interaction, after which it is discussed between the supervisor and supervisee. In this method the supervisor is able to obtain a clearer view of the process occurring between the supervisee and the patient. Live supervision, on the other hand, may foster dependence on the supervisor always to be there and giving the answers. This method may not always encourage independence in the supervisees.

CONCLUSION

The overall goal of supervision is to promote professional learning and development to provide safe patient care. Supervision must be characterised by a climate of trust and support, an ongoing and continuous process, and a shared responsibility between supervisors and supervisees. It should be based upon a collegial, collaborative philosophy that includes various approaches and individual input into methods and processes. Relevant information and observations should be shared between members of the multidisciplinary team on an ongoing basis, which includes access to any documentation taken during supervision.

SELF-ASSESSMENT

Before moving on to the next chapter, make sure that you can discuss the following key concepts and their application in your context with a colleague:

- The meaning of the word 'supervision'
- The purpose of being an effective supervisor
- The various methods of supervision
- The rights and responsibilities of the supervisor and supervisee.

CHAPTER TWO

Supervision: Roles, skills, types and styles

ROLES OF NURSE SUPERVISORS

Supervision should be available to all nurse practitioners, regardless of seniority. All supervisors should themselves receive regular supervision, in order to monitor and develop the quality of supervision.

Learning activity 4

Feedback on supervision of older people, friends and unions

During supervision many challenges face the supervisor.

Professional nurse Subina Moloi has just been appointed as a supervisor in the intensive care unit. She is surprised when she realises that some of her old friends and previous colleagues who are older than she is will be working with her. They all belong to the labour union.

Her colleagues could be upset that she was the successful candidate. Which strategies should she implement to address this complex situation? Write down your answer on page 36.

LEVELS OF SUPERVISORS

In a large nursing service the chief nursing service manager in charge of and responsible for the nursing service cannot personally supervise the rendering of care. Supervision is therefore delegated to other nursing managers and professional nurses.

Middle-level nursing managers include supervisors and chief professional nurses who supervise more than one unit or department.

Nurse supervisors are usually first-level nurses, who are appropriately qualified, experienced and have received some preparation for the role. They should coordinate the total nursing care given to patients/clients in the unit.

Table 2.1 distinguishes between some of the supervisory duties of an area supervisor and a first-line manager.

Table 2.1 Duties of supervisors at different levels

Duty	Middle-level supervisors	First-level supervisors
Planning	Participate in planning activities of units in their area and coordinate activities with all units to be in line with policies	Plan and coordinate activities in the unit
Directing	Direct senior professional nurses in carrying out their responsibilities in the management of nursing care towards attainment of the vision of the service	Direct the work of supervisees towards attaining the unit objectives
Communicating	Consult with unit managers on specific nursing problems and interpretation of policies in the service	Ensure two-way communication between themselves and supervisees
Evaluating	Monitor the performance of nurses in an area/department as a whole and suggest changes Inspect unit areas to verify that patient needs are met	Set realistically high standards that are based on professional competencies Observe and assess the work performances of unit members

The **roles** of a supervisor could include acting as a coach, consultant, mentor, role model, advocate, counsellor, and motivator in nursing practice.

Coach

A good supervisor places a high priority on coaching followers. Good coaching involves working with supervisees to establish suitable goals, action plans and time lines. The supervisor delegates and also provides ongoing guidance and support to supervisees as they complete their action plans. Rarely can job goals be established without considering other aspects of a supervisee's life, for example time available for training, career preferences, and personal strengths and weaknesses. A supervisor is sometimes confronted with walking a fine line between being a supervisor and the supervisee's confidante. The supervisor as coach should:

- Know when to coach by recognising the need for help when delegating, giving instructions or encouraging a supervisee to grow and develop
- Decide if a formal remedial coaching session is warranted, by establishing if there is really a problem where a supervisee is not meeting a performance standard
- Prepare for a coaching session, collect information, structure the message to suit the needs and experience of the supervisee, anticipate possible outcomes and reactions, and select a time and place for the session
- Agree on a need for change, for example the supervisee must agree on the exact nature of the problem, take all facts into consideration, as the definition of the problem of the supervisee and the supervisor may differ
- Agree on specific actions to be taken, the best options, measurable goals by which progress can be measured

- Establish and agree upon a schedule of review at the coaching sessions to ensure the plan of action is working
- Recap the actions you have agreed on and check for understanding
- Set a follow-up date to review the progress of the supervisee and to show the supervisee that you are willing to help if required.

Supervisees should be encouraged to reflect on the skills required to function effectively within their own nursing practice, and to identify areas for further development. Observation of supervisees in nursing practice is used to assist in the reflective process.

Observations reflected to supervisees of their nursing practice should be accurate, and improvements should be suggested. Where required, supervisees are referred to accepted protocols and best practice in the field. Development plans for each supervisee should be consistent with their identified learning needs and should provide specific, measurable, attainable, realistic and time-bound criteria and guidelines for activities to be completed.

Plans include personal and professional development plans. An understanding of the different ways in which people learn promotes diversity in own coaching and teaching, as well as providing learning opportunities to supervisees.

Strategies of coaching include feedback and self-awareness. Feedback includes involvement in programme development, staff development programmes, in-service training and structured reading. Self-awareness promotes identification of own bias and blind spots, and is helpful in creating an environment that allows for constructive feedback.

Consultant

A good consultant should undertake to do the following:
- Objectively assess problem situations
- Provide alternative interventions and/or conceptualisations of problems
- Facilitate supervisee brainstorming of alternatives
- Collaboratively develop strategies for supervisee growth.

Mentor

Usually the supervisor understands the organisation and the supervisee's profession better than the supervisee does. Consequently, the supervisor is in a unique position to give ongoing advice to supervisees about their job and career. Supervisees can look to the supervisor as a model for direction and development. An effective mentor–mentee relationship requires the supervisor to accept the responsibility of mentorship. A good supervisor can be a priceless addition to the career of a supervisee.

As a mentor, the supervisor can:
- Help new staff members to feel part of the unit and organisation
- Provide information about the way the unit operates

- Help staff members to set goals
- Listen to problems, calm fears, provide feedback, and boost the confidence of supervisees
- Act as a role model to observe competencies.

Role model

The competencies of a role model can be seen through:
- Inspiring change among supervisees
- Facilitating team spirit
- Showing enthusiasm in training supervisees
- Ensuring efficient planning and improvement in the unit
- Satisfying clients' needs
- Promoting effective problem-solving skills in groups
- Promoting quality service and participation among supervisees
- Using statistics as valuable tools for the development of supervisees
- Assessing quality systems
- Focusing on the auditing of records.

Learning activity 5
Role modelling

Complete the self-evaluation instrument on page 37 and determine in which role-modelling aspects you would still need development as a supervisor.

Advocate for the unit and organisation

Often, the supervisor is the first person to tell supervisees about new policies and programmes from management. It is not uncommon that supervisees are confused or frustrated by these new actions, and need further clarification and support from supervisors. In the rapidly changing world of today's organisations, it can be a major challenge to present new programmes to followers without them being frustrated or even cynical. The supervisor must be authentic, yet tactful.

Advocate for supervisee

The supervisor is often responsible for presenting the supervisee's requests to management, along with presenting the supervisee's case for deserving a reward. For example, if a supervisee deserves an incentive, the supervisor often has to justify the case for the incentive to the supervisor's supervisor, as well. If the supervisee has a rather outstanding performance appraisal report that warrants special consideration by the rest of management, the supervisor must explain this situation and how it can be handled. It is not unusual for supervisees to sometimes see the supervisor as part of 'management', while at other times sees the supervisor as a personal friend.

Counsellor

In terms of professional characteristics (roles and skills), excellent supervisors are knowledgeable and competent counsellors and supervisors. They have extensive training and wide experience in counselling, which have helped them achieve a broad perspective of the field. They can effectively employ a variety of supervision interventions, and deliberately choose from these interventions based on their assessment of a supervisee's learning needs, learning style, and personal characteristics. They seek ongoing growth in counselling and supervision through continuing education activities, self-evaluation, and feedback from supervisees, clients, other supervisors, and colleagues.

Counsellors are empathic, genuine, open and flexible in their approach. They respect their supervisees as individuals and as developing professionals, and are sensitive to individual differences (e.g. gender, race and ethnicity).

Motivator

A supervisor should motivate supervisees towards the vision of the whole organisation. Certain principles on how to motivate include the following:
- Understand the term motivation
- Focus on job enrichment
- Learn to like your followers
- Encourage participation in the unit
- Provide open communication in the unit
- Make work itself a motivator
- Lead the way by example
- Reward accomplishments
- Instil a desire to achieve goals
- Provide opportunities for growth in the unit.

Learning activity 6
Motivational principles and examples

Complete the Table on page 38 and give examples for each of the principles of motivation.

SKILLS NEEDED BY A SUPERVISOR

Communication and interpersonal skills

The supervisor should be able to listen attentively and actively, and to comment openly, objectively and constructively with patience. Sound interpersonal relationships should be maintained with followers and the demonstration of loyalty and mutual respect should be evident.

Ability to act professionally

Supervisors should demonstrate integrity through their behaviour. Sound, up-to-date knowledge in their field is essential according to their registration at the professional body that regulates practice. Self-motivation could inspire supervisees to have a sense of responsibility.

Supportive skills

Supervisors should be able to identify when support and caring are needed and offer supportive responses. Support could be visible through the implementation of management by objectives, and effective problem-solving and decision-making strategies. Problems should be handled fairly and objectively.

General and specialised skills

Specific knowledge of general nursing science is needed. Nurses who specialise in particular fields of work should have access to supervision by someone who is similarly oriented. Supervisors should also be able to meet with other supervisors, to continue to improve their own skills.

Learning activity 7
Skills in supervision

A supervisor is rarely perfect and needs skills in supervision. Supervisors can acquire bad habits that can irritate their staff members. Read the scenario below.

Supervisor Mary Tabondo has been the supervisor in a paediatric unit for more than five years. In the last year she has received complaints from her nursing team regarding her supervision skills. She calls a meeting to address their dissatisfaction. At this meeting the following six main complaints come to the fore:
- 'You are always too inaccessible.'
- 'You rarely compliment us on tasks we thought we had completed well.'
- 'You are out of touch with what is going on in the workplace.'
- 'You avoid making decisions.'
- 'You never seem to listen to what we are saying.'
- 'You have favourites.'

Reading through these comments, which principles do you identify as important to act as an effective supervisor? Write down your answers on page 38, after which you can read the feedback on pages 56–57.

After reading the roles of a supervisor above you should note that there is a paradigm shift in supervision. In the past, supervision was focused on policies and procedures, completing the right activities, focusing on technical skills, placing a high value on rigidity, controlling followers, job security and discipline. These aspects are still necessary; however, in an environment where there is a shortage of staff, supervisors should rather shift their thinking towards the following:

- Recognising the need to make judgements
- Focusing on obtaining the right objectives/results
- Using communication skills effectively
- Placing a high value on flexibility
- Motivating supervisees
- Providing career guidance
- Being a coach.

In this changing environment the role of the supervisor may become different, with more administrative and supervisory tasks, and less involvement with the work of the supervisees. Responsibilities will increase as supervisors are responsible for the work of others as well for their own performances.

TYPES OF SUPERVISION

Supervision is a multi-dimensional process. Identifying the types of supervision required should be carried out in conjunction with the supervisee, and in the light of their professional development and service requirements. All supervision should be continuously evaluated for effectiveness. For this type of supervision to be effective, there must be mutual trust and respect between supervisor and supervisee.

Supervision should cover the following four principal areas:

- Professional standards and evaluation of work performances
- Support
- Personal growth and development
- Clinical work.

These four principal areas are covered by the types of supervision described below.

Managerial supervision

Managerial supervision entails the promotion and maintenance of good standards of work, the monitoring of work and workload, assuring work and work completion, quality and quantity control, and appropriate implementation of institutional policies and procedures. The supervisor assures that the purpose, vision and policies of the institution are met through adherence to policies and good practice. One aspect of supervision is the quality assurance dimension and the other aspect is the 'community of practice' dimension, together ensuring that standards are maintained.

Managerial supervision will be addressed in Chapter 3.

Supportive supervision

This type of supervision provides support, understanding and assistance to supervisees, while understanding their emotional needs. Supervisors provide supervisees with a supportive environment where they can enjoy high morale and job satisfaction, as well as the practical and psychological support to carry through the responsibilities of their role. In supportive supervision the primary issue is morale and job satisfaction of staff members. The stresses and pressures of the coaching role can affect work performance and take its toll psychologically and physically. In extreme and prolonged situations these may ultimately lead to burnout. The supervisor's role is to help staff members manage their stress more effectively and provide re-assurance and emotional support. *The supportive element* builds on morale and job satisfaction at its basic level; it involves understanding, identifying stress factors that may affect the professional and may impinge on the client. At its extreme end it involves an assessment of whether practice is safe for the professional, the client and the agency.

Receiving supervision contributes significantly to the reduction of emotional exhaustion among nurses. If the experience of stress is not alleviated, the consequences for nurses are problems with maintaining standards and quality of care offered to patients.

Educational supervision

This entails the assessment of skills, evaluation of needs, provision of learning experiences, and upgrading of knowledge and skills. This type of supervision focuses on the educational development of the staff member and the fulfilment of potential. In educational supervision the primary issue is staff ignorance and/or ineptitude regarding the knowledge, attitude and skills required to do their job. The goal is to dispel ignorance and upgrade skills by encouraging reflection on and exploration of the work. *The educational element* encourages reflection on, and exploration of the work and of current research, evidence and policy. Supervisees are helped to understand the client better, be aware of their own responses, examine the dynamics of the relationship and evaluate their intervention. It involves exploring other ways of working through peer or agency knowledge and suggests further development through mentoring, reading or training to deliver on objectives.

Clinical supervision

One of the primary reasons for all supervision is to ensure that the quality of therapeutic intervention with the client is of a consistently high standard in relation to the client's needs. Consequently, supervision must be acknowledged as a cornerstone of clinical practice. Clinical supervision looks at the nurse's behaviour within the nurse–patient relationship. Clinical supervision is a model that must continue throughout professional life, thus providing a supporting as well as an educative purpose.

Learning activity 8

Characteristics of a supervisor

Professional Nurse Hester Magobe has been appointed in your ward as supervisor based on her outstanding performance appraisal. She has the following characteristics:

she is 35 years old, has been in the health-care service for three years, has never been a supervisor before and has undergone tertiary education.

Reading through this profile, which of these characteristics are often found among supervisors in the unit? Write your answer down on page 39.

STYLES IN SUPERVISION

The managerial, educational and functional types of supervision are always evident in supervision, however, the extent to which the supervisor uses these styles may differ as the supervisee becomes more competent. The styles of the supervisor can be viewed on a continuum of supervision (see Figure 2.1), where the supervisor moves her/his focus with the supervisee from normative, to formative and then to the restorative style of supervision.

Phase 1: **Normative.** The supervisor accepts (or more accurately shares with the supervisee) responsibility for ensuring that the supervisee's work is professional and ethical, operating within whatever codes, laws and organisational norms apply (directive style).

Phase 2: **Formative.** The supervisor acts to provide feedback or direction that will enable the supervisee to develop the skills, theoretical knowledge, personal attributes, and so on that will mean the supervisee becomes an increasingly competent practitioner (collaborative).

Phase 3: **Restorative.** The supervisor is there to listen, support and confront the supervisee when the inevitable personal issues, doubts and insecurities arise (consultative).

Careful consideration should be given to the qualifications, skills and experience required of supervisors, and to their ability to meet the individual needs of the supervisees. All supervisees should also have the opportunity to receive training and learn skills that are constructive and supportive. All supervisors should have the same opportunity to learn about their role.

Phase of supervision	Normative	Formative	Restorative
Supervision needed	Active	Transitional	Self-supervision
Style of supervisor	Directive	Collaborative	Consultative

Figure 2.1 Continuum of supervision

In Phase 1 supervisors use a directive style and play an active role in evaluating the guidance needed by the supervisee in the policies and procedures of the unit. Continuous feedback should be given to the supervisee to develop professional skills and judgement in order to improve the standards of service.

In Phase 2 the style is more collaborative because transition takes place from being a novice to a more competent supervisee.

Phase 3 represents more competent supervisees who are able to evaluate their own performances. In this phase, the style of the supervisor is more consultative.

Specific characteristics and needs are identified at various developmental stages of the supervisee, and the supervisor thus has different tasks and responsibilities in accordance with the supervisee's stage. In addition, supervisors develop dimensions such as competency, autonomy, identity and self-awareness throughout their supervisory career.

Tips on principles to be followed in supervision

- Supervisees must understand clearly what is expected of them.
- Supervisees must have guidance in doing their work on how to listen, speak, read, write, organise work, schedule activities and conduct meetings.
- Good work should always be recognised through, for example, praise.
- Poor performance of supervisees requires constructive criticism.
- People should always have the opportunity to show that they can accept greater responsibility.
- People should be encouraged to improve themselves through using creativity and determination.

CONCLUSION

Supervisors ensure that new supervisees orient themselves to the organisation, its policies, facilities, etc. They develop training plans with supervisees to ensure that they have the necessary expertise to carry out their jobs. They provide ongoing guidance to supervisees, often in the form of ongoing coaching and counselling. Supervisors often provide career counselling to help supervisees develop and advance in their careers.

SELF-ASSESSMENT

Before moving on to the next chapter, make sure that you can discuss the following key concepts and their application in your context with a colleague:
- The various roles a supervisor should play in a unit
- The differences between the types of supervision
- The skills an effective supervisor should possess.

CHAPTER THREE

Managerial supervision

A summary of the scope of managerial supervision was given in Chapter 2. This aspect of the supervisor's role is clear when a line management relationship exists. The *administrative element* ensures that agency policy is implemented but also enables supervisees to work to the best of their ability. This quality assurance function is in the interests of the client and institution as much as the professional.

Managerial supervision on its own could possibly over-emphasise standards at the expense of support. Managers have a disciplinary role, which may influence the supervisees' willingness to share aspects of themselves. This type of supervision can ensure that standards are maintained and developed. Non-managerial supervision is able to identify skills development and offer support, but may have little influence on poor standards.

Supervisors have many responsibilities in managerial supervision.

HUMAN RESOURCES MANAGEMENT

The supervisor is responsible for liaison with the Human Resources Department. The Human Resources (HR) Department guides and supports activities in staffing, development and management of personnel policies and records, training and development, performance appraisals and performance problems, career counselling and organisational development. HR assists the supervisor and provides help to ensure that all human resources activities conform to relevant laws, rules and regulations.

Personnel policies and procedures

The supervisor is usually responsible for ensuring that supervisees follow the organisation's policies and procedures, for example for sick time, personal leave, overtime, contact with the media or press and confidentiality about organisational information. Concurrently, the supervisor must follow the policies and procedures for carrying out supervisory responsibilities, for example policies and procedures for appointments, dismissal and promotions.

Staffing

Supervisors regularly review the needs of their supervisees. Consequently, they are often the first to notice the need for a new position in the organisation. The supervisor opens a new post by getting authorisation from upper management. This often requires communication and justification for funds to fill the new position. The supervisor reviews advertisements for job candidates, reviews résumés and conducts interviews. The supervisor recommends who should be hired from among job candidates and ensures a job offer is made to the most suitable candidate. There is usually a great deal of paperwork, for example a job application, starting a personnel file, providing a supervisee manual, salary and tax forms, etc. Finally, the supervisor must ensure that the supervisee has adequate facilities and supplies.

Training and development of supervisees

Supervisors ensure that new supervisees are oriented to the organisation, its policies, facilities, etc. They develop training plans with supervisees to ensure that they have the necessary expertise to carry out their jobs. They provide ongoing guidance to supervisees, often in the form of ongoing coaching and counselling. Supervisors often provide career counselling, to help supervisees develop and advance in their careers.

Performance management of supervisees

Supervisee performance management can be viewed as part of managerial supervision. Supervisors ensure that job descriptions accurately record the primary responsibilities, qualifications and terms for each role in their unit. They set performance standards for the tasks, jobs and roles of their supervisees. They ensure that supervisees have appropriate and realistic job goals. They provide ongoing feedback about the supervisee's performance. They conduct performance appraisals on a regular basis, including assessing how supervisees have performed and what they can do to improve in their jobs. They develop performance improvement plans if a supervisee's performance is not adequate. In addition, supervisors provide rewards for supervisee accomplishments.

Supervision gives us the means to develop professional skills and judgement, and a commitment to achieving professional growth in order to improve the standards of service.

Evaluation of managerial supervision

Supervisors should assess their unit for strengths and weaknesses in human and financial resources that could affect the service delivery to clients negatively.

Learning activity 9
Quality assurance measures

An evaluation instrument for managerial supervision is essential. The supervisor should have a tool to measure the extent to which aspects regarding the implementation of policies and procedures in the unit are problematic.

Complete the instrument on pages 40–43 and determine to what extent these aspects are fully complied with in nursing practice.

After using the instrument the supervisor should do a situation analysis to determine which aspects need attention (see Table 3.1).

Table 3.1 Analysis of some shortcomings in the unit

Aspect	Strengths	Weaknesses
Human resources	Experts in the field of speciality	Absenteeism
Financial resources	Effective cost-control policy	Poor recording of used supplies
Policies	Policy manual up to date	Policy on overtime not followed
Patient satisfaction	An evaluation tool for patient satisfaction is in place	Feedback of patients is not always made known
Interpersonal relationships	An ethical code of conduct exists to guide supervisees in promoting interpersonal relationships	Conflicts in the unit are badly managed
Staff development	An in-service training programme exists	Staff members do not attend scheduled sessions

Supervisors should have at least a monthly plan, in line with the strategic plan of the service, to implement supervisory actions needed. An example of this plan is provided in Table 3.2.

Table 3.2 Plan to address weaknesses in the unit

Shortcomings in Ward B	Objectives	Actions	Person responsible	Due date
Absenteeism	To promote effective use of human resources			
Poor recording of used supplies	Cost-effectiveness in the utilisation of supplies			
Policy on overtime not followed	To implement policies effectively			
Feedback of patients is not always made known	To address the problems clients experience in the unit			
Conflicts in the unit are badly managed	To promote interpersonal relationships in the unit			
Staff members do not attend scheduled sessions	To encourage staff development of staff members			

Learning activity 10

Weaknesses in the unit

Read Table 3.2 above and indicate the actions you would implement to address the weaknesses in this unit, on page 44.

CONCLUSION

Managerial supervision ensures that the purpose, vision and policies of the institution are met through adherence to policies and good practice. It is therefore a quality assurance dimension of supervision.

SELF-ASSESSMENT

Before moving on to the next chapter, make sure that you can discuss the following key concepts and their application in your context with a colleague:
* The responsibilities of managerial supervision
* Means to evaluate managerial supervision in your unit.

CHAPTER FOUR

Clinical supervision

The role/responsibility of the supervisor is to provide a safe environment in which the supervisee can work through the developmental issues or challenges in order to gain the necessary motivation, autonomy and self-awareness to successfully move to the next level of development.

GUIDELINES FOR CLINICAL SUPERVISION

In clinical supervision certain guidelines should be taken into consideration:
- Ensure that the actions/steps associated with the accomplishment of specific tasks by supervisees are relevant.
- Analyse the tasks to identify and evaluate the hazards in terms of safety measures (personal protective equipment, training).
- Evaluate if supervisees are qualified to perform the job, for example: Do they know how to perform the job? Have requirements for training been determined?
- Schedule, coordinate, direct and discuss all aspects of the tasks while providing details.
- Evaluate supervisees' performance by observation and communication with the supervisees and the clients/patients.
- Adjust (where necessary) procedures for future task requirements.
- Have actions in place to evaluate overall performance of staff members over time.
- Set performance standards for supervisees (ensure quantifiable objectives), evaluate their behaviour, discuss performance indicators with them (strengths, weaknesses, improvement needed), and initiate awards or disciplinary measures as appropriate.

Developmental approach

During clinical supervision a developmental approach is followed (Pierce & Rowell, 2005:4). The objectives and actions that are recommended for a developmental approach in clinical supervision are shown below.

Objectives	Actions
Establish two-way communication	Ensure active listening and be transparent
Create an atmosphere of hope and confidence	Provide opportunities to succeed and have high expectations for supervisees

Objectives	Actions
Allow autonomy of supervisees	Provide appropriate delegation Encourage risk taking
Uphold individual responsibility	Create a culture where staff hold each other and themselves accountable
Set high expectations for staff members	Provide clear position descriptions Hold regular feedback sessions with staff
Provide praise and encouragement	Ensure formal recognition systems and informal compliments when observing they are doing things right
Promote a team spirit and be available and accessible to supervisees	Provide an open door policy Hold regular one-on-one supervisory meetings
Provide support for supervisees' professional growth and development	Develop professional development plans and performance appraisal systems
Promote ownership	Create opportunities for employees to contribute in participatory strategic planning sessions
Reinforce relationships	Get to know what motivates individual supervisees Create opportunities for them to share personal accomplishments

While implementing the principles of clinical supervision, supervisors should monitor the supervisee in nursing practice. A needs assessment can be performed to evaluate the needs of supervisees in delivering nursing care.

Learning activity 11
Combating negligence in the unit

Complete the needs assessment on pages 44–46 to determine the extent to which supervisees require clinical supervision in nursing care delivery.

The reason for evaluating the competencies of supervisees in nursing practice is to ensure quality, safe nursing practice.

PREVENTION OF NEGLIGENT SUPERVISION

A major responsibility in clinical supervision is to prevent negligence in patient care. The absence of appropriate supervision could have serious consequences. The following are examples of sentences of the disciplinary hearing committee of the South African Nursing Council (SANC), regarding negligence in supervision of professional nurses that led to inadequate patient care by their supervisees (professional and sub-professional categories):

- Negligently inflicted an injury to the patient resulting in the loss of the left arm
- Willfully made acts of sexual advancement to a professional nurse, who was under supervision whilst on night duty

- Negligently failed to observe, assess, monitor and evaluate the condition of a very ill patient
- Negligently failed to carry out a medical practitioner's prescribed orders for a patient
- Negligently failed to maintain a safe environment for the patient
- Negligently failed to seek the intervention of a medical practitioner when the patient's condition warranted such intervention
- Wrongfully acted beyond the scope of practice by prescribing Valium 10 mg tablets to the relatives of a deceased patient
- Negligently failed to ensure the proper safekeeping of scheduled medication
- Negligently failed to act promptly in preparing the patient for the operating theatre who was booked for an emergency caesarean section
- Negligently delayed an emergency transfer of a patient's baby to a regional hospital as per doctor's instruction
- Wrongfully administered Schedule seven medication to a patient without a legal prescription.

Learning activity 12
Professional behaviour

A case of negligence in clinical supervision can, apart from being heard at SANC, also be heard in the civil court, when a patient makes a civil case against a professional nurse. Read examples of parts of a report on negligence in clinical supervision that could serve in such a court hearing on pages 46–48.

After reading some examples of the transcript of the report, you should identify aspects of clinical supervision that were lacking in that case.

CONCLUSION

Good supervisors are able to function effectively in the roles of teacher, counsellor and consultant, making informed choices about which role to employ at any given time with a particular supervisee. In clinical practice nursing supervisors should be aware that the safety of the patient is their first concern, and therefore should accompany their supervisees toward competent practice in delivering nursing care.

SELF-ASSESSMENT

Before moving on to the next chapter, make sure that you can discuss the following key concepts and their application in your context with a colleague:
- The most important principles of clinical supervision
- Which aspects it is necessary for the supervisor to monitor in order to deliver good patient care
- Negligence in nursing care due to poor clinical supervision.

CHAPTER FIVE

Evaluation and supervision

Throughout this book, many aspects of supervision have been evaluated.

What should be mentioned is that supervisors have to supervise and evaluate the adequate *functioning of the unit, as well as themselves.*

Five important dimensions can be assesed to evaluate the effectiveness of a supervisor:

- Communication between the supervisor and the person being supervised
- Positive reputation of the supervisor
- Personal attributes and styles
- Nurturing attitude towards supervisees
- Knowledge and experience in supervision.

The effectiveness of the supervisor could be determined by the supervisees as well as by self-evaluation. Certain indicators of an effective–ineffective supervisor role could be evaluated.

Learning activity 13
Evaluating own shortcomings

Complete the instrument on pages 49–50 to show your effectiveness as a supervisor. Use the following scale in completing the activity:

Scale: 1 = Highly effective
        2 = Effective
        3 = Less than effective
        4 = Ineffective supervisor

You have completed evaluation instruments relating to managerial and clinical supervision. Another handy tool is the support list. A support list is a tool to remind you to systematically review important aspects related to supervision in a unit. It could consist of three sections, namely a red flag section, a regular review section and a quarterly supervisory support section. Some aspects to be supervised are given in Table 5.1 on the following page.

Table 5.1 Example of a supervision support list

Ward name	January		February		March	
HIGH IMPORTANCE						
No staff not on duty						
Sick leave						
Professional nurses absent number of days without leave						
Non-professional nurses absent number of days without leave						
No broken equipment						
Glucometer						
Baumenometer						
Scale						
No incident reports						
Written						
Not written						
Lack of supplies						
Drug supplies						
Linen						
Emergency equipment						
Emergency trolley equipment						
ACTIONS TO BE TAKEN						
REGULAR IMPORTANCE						
Staffing	January		February		March	
Leave forms complete	Yes	No	Yes	No	Yes	No
Staff meetings took place	Yes	No	Yes	No	Yes	No
Staff attended training	Yes	No	Yes	No	Yes	No
ACTIONS TO BE TAKEN						
Routine	January		February		March	
Fridge temp correct	Yes	No	Yes	No	Yes	No
Sharps disposal correct	Yes	No	Yes	No	Yes	No

Drug supplies adequate	Yes	No	Yes	No	Yes	No
Monthly stocktaking	Yes	No	Yes	No	Yes	No
Drug book entries checked	Yes	No	Yes	No	Yes	No
Statistical return correct	Yes	No	Yes	No	Yes	No
ACTIONS TO BE TAKEN						
New projects initiated	Yes	No	Yes	No	Yes	No
ACTIONS TO BE TAKEN						

QUARTERLY IMPORTANCE	1st QUARTER		ACTIONS TO BE TAKEN
Staffing			
Number of vacant posts			
Number of disciplinary actions pending			
Number of staff reports outstanding			
Draw staff training plan	Yes	No	
Plan weekly meeting	Yes	No	
Support services			
Repairs outstanding	Yes	No	
Statistics			
Record system correct	Yes	No	

Learning activity 14

Staff development role

The last activity in this book on supervision is the ward round. Many examples of such instruments exist, however, it is important that you have an instrument for your own unit that includes all the relevant aspects to be monitored and evaluated during a ward round. This instrument should also be used as a teaching tool for students in training.

Do a ward round with one of your students and complete the ward round tool on pages 50–52.

SUMMARY

At this stage, you should have realised that acting as a nursing supervisor is a multi-faceted approach that includes a large range of responsibilities and accountability. In supervising your unit, you act within a specific legal and ethical framework, play various roles and functions, which includes planning, monitoring and evaluating the unit activities for the benefit of patients.

Worksheets for learning activities

Learning activity 1
Bookmark on supervision

Write down your top 10 reasons for supervising a student nurse in your unit.

BOOKMARK

Top 10 reasons to supervise a student nurse
1 ....
2 ....
3 ....
4 ....
5 ....
6 ....
7 ....
8 ....
9 ....
10 ....

See an example of reasons to guide a supervisee on page 53.

Learning activity 2
Scenario

The supervisor in the scenario had to fulfil her responsibilities in meeting the purposes of supervision. Give examples or reasons why you think the sister in charge did not act as an effective supervisor in the scenario you read.

For example:
Professional learning and development and teaching the supervisee
A newly appointed first-year student should be oriented on bed and pressure parts, and the supervisor should monitor her/his care delivery.

Protecting the welfare and best interest of the client

....

....

....

Giving support to team members

....

....

....

Providing the supervisee with a safe, protective relationship in which to be creative

....

....

....

Monitoring the supervisee's performance and development

....

....

....

Improving own supervisory skills

....

....

....

Ensuring quality assurance in service delivery

....

....

....

Read some possible answers on this activity on pages 53–54.

Learning activity 3
Supervisory contract

Below is an example for a supervisory contract document.

Ward	Month and year
Expectations	
Supervisor	**Supervisee**
Responsibilities	
Signature	**Signature**
Date	**Date**

After compiling this contract, make sure that you included the necessary aspects as stipulated on page 54.

Learning activity 4
Feedback on supervision of older people, friends and unions

Older people:

....

....

Friends:

....

....

Union:

....

....

Overall the supervisor should:

....

....

After you have stipulated your answers, turn to page 54 for further possible answers.

Learning activity 5
Role modelling

Complete the instrument below.

AT PRESENT				ROLE MODELLING	SHOULD BE			
Never	Sometimes	Regularly	Always	**The supervisor ...** 1 = Never 2 = Sometimes 3 = Regularly 4 = Always	Never	Sometimes	Regularly	Always
1	2	3	4	Sets an example by doing what she/he expects others to do, e.g. coming on duty on time.	1	2	3	4
1	2	3	4	Implements the supervisees' suggestions that contribute to the effective functioning of clinic activities.	1	2	3	4
1	2	3	4	Applies her/his communication skills to better the functioning of the clinic nursing team.	1	2	3	4
1	2	3	4	Demonstrates self-confidence as a member of the disciplinary team.	1	2	3	4
1	2	3	4	Accepts accountability for all her/his conduct/behaviour and decision-making in the clinic.	1	2	3	4
1	2	3	4	Does *not* need praise from others regarding her/his day-to-day performance/conduct.	1	2	3	4
1	2	3	4	Acts as a buffer and protects the supervisee against internal and negative work factors that can lead to more tension or work overload.	1	2	3	4
1	2	3	4	Reflects a positive image towards the supervisee.	1	2	3	4
1	2	3	4	Acknowledges the nursing team for their contribution to the success of, e.g. an open day, and does not take all the credit for her/himself.	1	2	3	4
1	2	3	4	Is humble enough to admit if she/he does not have the relevant information/knowledge.	1	2	3	4
1	2	3	4	Shows that her/his position does not make her/him a better person than others, e.g. she/he does not talk down to the supervisee.	1	2	3	4
1	2	3	4	Stays in touch with the supervisees' needs through ongoing evaluation of their progress.	1	2	3	4

After completing the instrument, read the comments on page 54.

Learning activity 6
Motivational principles and examples

Give examples for each of the motivational principles to be followed by a supervisor in a unit.

Motivational principles	Your examples
Understand the term motivation	
Focus on job enrichment	
Learn to like your supervisees	
Encourage participation in the unit	
Provide open communication in the unit	
Make work itself a motivator	
Lead the way by example	
Reward accomplishments	
Instil a desire to achieve goals	
Provide opportunities for growth in the unit	

After completing Learning activity 6, you may turn to pages 55–56 to read some more possible examples of these motivational principles.

Learning activity 7
Skills in supervision

Write down the required skills of a supervisor that you believe are necessary in a scenario where there are complaints about your supervisory expertise.

....

....

....

....

....

....

....

Now read the possible answers on pages 56–57.

Learning activity 8

Characteristics of a supervisor

After reading the brief scenario on page 19, write down the most important characteristic a supervisor's appointment should be based on. Use the following headings:

Performance appraisal: ....

What age: ....

Years in the service: ....

Experience as a supervisor: ....

....

....

Previous training: ....

....

....

After completing your ideas, read the comments on page 57.

Learning activity 9

Quality assurance measures

Complete the following instrument in the unit in which you are appointed and determine the extent to which managerial supervision is complied with in these aspects.

Evaluation tool for aspects of managerial supervision (NC = Non-Compliant; PC = Partially Compliant; C = Compliant)	NC	PC	C
Nursing care delivery takes place within the legislative/professional framework of the nursing profession			
The Nursing Act No 33 of 2005 (with amendments and regulations) is available in the unit.			
Other relevant Acts and Regulations specific to the unit setting are available.			
The nursing staff practise within their own abilities and qualifications and accept accountability for their own nursing care and service delivery.			
Nursing staff members are functioning in accordance with common law and the constitution of the country.			
Staff accept accountability for service delivery, in accordance with standards and policies of the health-care service.			
Staff use the nursing process to deliver comprehensive care to patients/clients.			
There is evidence of support for the management of ethical problems experienced by nursing staff.			
Actions to be taken on limitations identified: Please fill in			
There are written updated policies and procedures in the unit			
• Management and administration of medication			
• Ordering of stocks and supplies			
• Personnel allocation			
There is a written unit organogram.			
The scheduling of shifts is based on the needs of patients and staff, according to a written policy.			
Planned unit meetings take place to address problems related to for example, cost-effectiveness and personnel management.			
Actions to be taken on limitations identified: Please fill in			
The unit is managed in accordance with the strategic plan of the particular health care service			
The nursing staff have a clear vision of the service rendered by the unit.			
The philosophy and mission of the institution are met.			
The unit has a plan that fits the strategic plan of the service.			

Evaluation tool for aspects of managerial supervision (NC = Non-Compliant; PC = Partially Compliant; C = Compliant)	NC	PC	C
The unit has measurable and attainable written objectives that are specifically related to the unit.			
Staff identify priorities to be addressed within the strategic plan of the service.			
Long- and short-term objectives are set in the strategic plan of the unit.			
New staff members are oriented on the strategic plan of the service.			
Actions to be taken on limitations identified: Please fill in			
There is a clear staffing process to be followed in the unit			
Well-written policies on personnel provision and utilisation are in place, e.g. promotion, transfer, termination of services, health and safety.			
There is a scientific system for establishing the nursing staff required to deliver the service.			
There is a formal system in place to verify the credentials of all full-time, part-time and agency staff.			
The unit manager participates in the nursing personnel selection process.			
There is a written orientation programme for new staff that is recorded.			
Responsibilities and authority of every post in the unit are outlined.			
Job specifications and descriptions are written for staff members.			
Strategies are used to enable different staff members to learn from one another's diversity, to develop cultural competence, and are appropriate to staff component and levels of expertise.			
A formal written grievance procedure is in place and followed.			
A formal disciplinary hearing procedure is in place.			
Staffing is according to the Labour Relations Act and other human resources legislation.			
The nursing unit manager practises participative management in the unit.			
Actions to be taken on limitations identified: Please fill in			
Communication networks are sufficient in the unit			
Communication that facilitates nursing teamwork and interdisciplinary collaboration is established and maintained.			
Lines of authority and communication are established.			
Actions to be taken on limitations identified: Please fill in			
Performance management is a continuous process in the unit			
Performance appraisals of staff members are conducted in a manner that reflects an understanding of new and experienced nurses and their differing needs.			
Acceptable standards for work performances are written.			

Evaluation tool for aspects of managerial supervision (NC = Non-Compliant; PC = Partially Compliant; C = Compliant)	NC	PC	C
The responsibilities of staff are available in writing by means of job descriptions.			
A formal system exists for the assignment of daily responsibilities of nursing care, e.g. duty lists.			
Specific time schedules for certain routine interactions exist.			
Nursing care assignment method(s) facilitate quality nursing care in the unit, e.g. functional, team, case, primary assignments.			
Delegation of duties are according to the general principles of delegation.			
Work division is fair and based on the competencies of staff and their need for personal and professional development.			
Performance appraisal follows the approved format of the institution.			
Punctuality of staff is monitored.			
Work procedures are updated according to changing circumstances.			
Work procedures take account of reality and are modified if necessary.			
Actions to be taken on limitations identified: Please fill in			
Adequate facilities, supplies and equipment are in place			
Standardisation of supplies and specifications exists.			
A policy is in place for replacement of equipment.			
Ordering of stocks, supplies and equipment takes place in a prescribed manner.			
An inventory system is in place.			
Equipment and supplies are placed in the correct area for maximum use.			
A system is in place to facilitate the mobilisation and accessing of the appropriate resources in the interest of patient care.			
The coordination of work and projects is logical.			
Health care is provided for the patient in a cost-effective manner in the interest of the service and the patient.			
Actions to be taken on limitations identified: Please fill in			
People management is adequately exercised			
The general principles of leadership are practised by the unit manager.			
There is a formalised communication system in the unit.			
There is a motivational and teambuilding strategy for the nursing staff in the unit to facilitate quality of work life/job satisfaction among the staff.			
Conflict management is appropriately managed.			
There is evidence of appropriate career planning of nursing staff.			
Actions to be taken on limitations identified: Please fill in			

Evaluation tool for aspects of managerial supervision (NC = Non-Compliant; PC = Partially Compliant; C = Compliant)	NC	PC	C
Quality improvement programmes are implemented in the unit			
A nursing audit process is in place to ensure adequate record-keeping.			
A safe environment for the patients is in place.			
Noise levels are monitored.			
There is an formal disaster plan in the unit.			
A formalised infection control programme/system is in place.			
A formal risk management programme for patients is in place.			
Actions to be taken on limitations identified: Please fill in			
Control measures are in place in the unit			
A standardised record system is in place for recording patient progress, diagnosis and treatment.		,	
The nursing record system complies with legal requirements.			
A reporting procedure for accidents and other incidents is followed.			
Medico-legal hazards and negative incidents are monitored and reported.			
An information system is in place to inform the unit manager about budgetary aspects, standards of care, reports.			
An appropriate handover procedure is followed.			
There is a system to manage professional conduct and accountability by nursing staff in the unit.			
The nursing manager is responsible for the management of the unit budget.			
A cost-containment process is followed in the unit.			
A formalised equipment control system is in place (inventory and maintenance).			
A formalised stock and supplies control system is in place.			
Actions to be taken on limitations identified: Please fill in			
Research findings and knowledge management are implemented in the unit setting			
Staff participate in action research and policy development within the practice setting.			
Staff maintain contemporary nursing knowledge.			
There is evidence of appropriate in-service education of staff.			
Actions to be taken on limitations identified: Please fill in			

After completing this activity and the actions to be taken to address the limitations, read the brief comment on page 57.

Learning activity 10
Weaknesses in the unit

Complete this needs assessment to address the weaknesses in this unit.

Shortcomings in Ward B	Objectives	Actions	Person responsible	Due date
Absenteeism	To promote effective use of human resources			
Poor recording of used supplies	Cost-effectiveness in the utilisation of supplies			
Policy on overtime not followed	To implement policies effectively			
Feedback of patients is not always made known	To address the problems clients experience in the unit			
Conflicts in the unit are badly managed	To promote interpersonal relationships in the unit			
Staff members do not attend scheduled sessions	To encourage staff development of staff members			

Now read pages 57–58 for some possible solutions that could be implemented to address these problems.

Learning activity 11
Combating negligence in the unit

A needs assessment: Evaluation of needs for clinical supervision
The unit manager can use this tool to identify clinical learning needs of the supervisee, and fill in actions to address shortcomings.

What is the extent to which supervisees need clinical supervision in nursing care?

To what extent do nursing staff: 1 = no extent 2 = small extent 3 = moderate extent 4 = full extent	1	2	3	4	Actions to be taken
Practise within the ethical framework of the nursing profession					
Follow the ethical principles and the professional code of ethics in health-care service delivery					
Practise the principles of scientifically based nursing care					
Ensure safe storage of the clients' valuables					
Nursing process					
Identify the patient using the correct procedure					
Implement nursing methods and procedures allocated to them correctly					
Promote multi-professional and multi-disciplinary teamwork and networking in the interest of patient care					
Appropriately refer the patient to other members of the health team					
Perform nursing assessments adequately in terms of risk assessment and mental state examinations of the patient					
Liaise with the doctor regarding discharge planning					
Patient and family involvement					
Gather information from relatives/carers who accompany the patient to hospital					
Maintain a constant safe environment for clients based on their risk assessment					
Patient education					
Orientate the client to the ward environment and daily routine					
Ensure clients are provided with written statements of their 'rights and responsibilities'					
Provide an explanation of and ensure patients' understanding of rights and responsibilities					
Planning of patient care					
Ensure that patients are aware of, understand and are involved in their treatment plan					
Ensure treatments and procedures are completed, i.e. X-rays, blood specimens, preparation for theatre					

To what extent do nursing staff: 1 = no extent 2 = small extent 3 = moderate extent 4 = full extent	1	2	3	4	Actions to be taken
Implementation of the nursing plan					
Deliver comprehensive nursing care to patients within the practice setting					
Administer prescribed medication correctly					
Provide ongoing monitoring and reporting of patients' mental and physical health status					
Monitor the observations of patients timeously					
Complete the daily score card of the health status of patients					
Need direction and supervision in the care of their patients					
Provide education and counselling towards the promotion of the health status improvements of patients within the practice setting					
Evaluate nursing care					
Nursing staff summarise the decisions made in the ward round and document the nursing care plan as soon as possible after the ward round					
Complete the necessary discharge records					
Ensure that appropriate plans are in place to facilitate patients' return to their community					

You have completed the instrument and should note that aspects rated 3 and lower need urgent attention in supervision.

Learning activity 12
Professional behaviour

When a case of negligence in clinical supervision is taken up in a civil court, an expert is required to give a report on the case. The following scenario is an example of a report that could be written by an expert. Read it carefully to identify the aspects in which clinical supervision was lacking.

Report of an expert

For purposes of completing the report, the following nursing records were consulted:

- The partogram
- A prescription/administration chart
- An antenatal progress report.

The nurse was an enrolled midwife. A midwife should act within the Scope of Practice of an enrolled midwife (according to the relevant Regulation of SANC).

The mother was dilated 2 cm at 8h30. Any qualified midwife should know this is active labour (second pregnancy) and should have started to monitor at least hourly observations on the partogram. The partogram was not correctly drawn with the relevant three lines to enable the enrolled nurse to establish the progress of labour.

Without a complete partogram the enrolled midwife could not effectively monitor the progress of labour as part of her scope of practice. The progress of labour and recorded observations on the partogram could have led to the decision to call the doctor and to prevent complications relating to labour.

The enrolled midwife did not check and monitor the mother and child at reasonable hourly intervals, doing this could have led to the correct diagnostic and therapeutic interventions.

A midwife should herself observe and record the vital signs of a mother and child.

The fact that the mother complained of low blood pressure and felt weak was not recorded.

The partogram did not indicate hourly observations of mother and child from 8h30 up to delivery after 14h00. The observations of the mother regarding blood pressure, pulse, temperature, urine tests and urine output were absent. The blood pressure was very important after an epidural treatment done by a doctor at 10h30. The fetal heart rate should have been continuously monitored after fetal distress was observed and recorded in the progress report around 12h20.

At 09h30 the enrolled midwife recorded in the progress report frequent painful contractions of 3–4 per 10 minutes. At 10h30 frequent moderate contractions were mentioned in the progress report but not on the partogram (number of contractions per minute absent). The records did not indicate the poor contractions that justified the introduction of Syntocinon IV.

At 11h00 the doctor saw the mother and was satisfied with the progress of the mother and baby. Between 10h50 and 12h30 no observations were recorded on the partogram. It is unclear which observations guided the enrolled midwife to start the 5E Syntocinon in the drip at 12h00 and continue to increase the dosage. On which observations did she make her decision? Infrequent but moderate contractions were reported in the progress report at 12h00 but it is unclear exactly what that meant.

At 12h20 the progress report stated that there was no slowing down of the fetal heart. This is not written in all normal maternity case records, and the fact that it is recorded in the patient progress reports therefore indicates that the midwife was aware of the fetal rate dropping at times.

At 12h30 strong contractions were recorded on the partogram, so why was the content of the Syntocinon drip further increased at 12h40 with the mother calling out and complaining of severe pain? The uterus was perhaps overstimulated and the drip should have been stopped.

The enrolled midwife recorded the fetal rate dropping at 12h40 in the progress report, but did not inform the doctor and still continued with the IV Syntocinon. At 13h00 the Syntocinon was further increased with a dropping fetal heart rate and the client was prepared for a normal delivery.

An abnormal fetal heart rate was evident; however, no frequent fetal heart rate observations were done by the enrolled midwife up to delivery. This scenario continued until about 14h00 without the doctor being informed about the situation.

The enrolled midwife did not observe and diagnose the seriousness of the fetal distress. The records do not indicate any concern regarding severe uterine contractions or the condition of the baby. The enrolled midwife did not exercise the specific care and treatment of this vulnerable mother and child.

The doctor should have been informed of the progress of the mother and child, which could have led to an emergency caesarean and an uncomplicated labour process. In accordance with the requirements of the circumstances and the seriousness of the mother and child's condition, the enrolled midwife should have referred the patient for medical care and not delayed such referral. She should have done what she could to promote the health status of the mother and child.

The enrolled midwife did not fulfil her role in effective advocacy to enable the mother and child to obtain the health care they needed.

It is not recorded that the enrolled midwife informed the mother of the reason for her decision to start with the Syntocinon drip.

Having read this example of a report, describe what the role of the nursing supervisor should have been in this case:

....

....

....

....

....

....

....

Learning activity 13
Evaluating own shortcomings

Indicate your answer by placing a cross (X) closest to the concept that describes your supervisor.

Large experience base			Small experience base
1	2	3	4

Encouraging			No encouragement given
1	2	3	4

Facilitator of learning			Uncertain of role
1	2	3	4

Resourceful			Not resourceful
1	2	3	4

Committed to supervisee			No interest in supervisee
1	2	3	4

Multidisciplinary			No encouragement given
1	2	3	4

Directed by supervisee's needs			Driven by self-needs
1	2	3	4

Highly organised			Lacks supervision experience
1	2	3	4

Positive self-image			Low self-image
1	2	3	4

Expert in research			Lacks research experience
1	2	3	4

Good writer   Not good at writing

| 1 | 2 | 3 | 4 |

Insightful   Neophyte

| 1 | 2 | 3 | 4 |

Intelligent   Ill-equipped

| 1 | 2 | 3 | 4 |

Knows what he/she wants   Does not know what he/she wants

| 1 | 2 | 3 | 4 |

Supportive   Judgemental

| 1 | 2 | 3 | 4 |

Learning activity 14
Staff development role

The following aspects are inspected and in order	✓	Needs attention
Office and nursing station		
Medicines (administration, storage, control of scheduled substances, expiry dates, surplus, storage cupboards/trolleys, pharmacy system in-out)		
Telephone system (lists, directions, security, verbal prescriptions)		
Standard forms and records (blood transfusion, doctor protocols, prescriptions and directions, consent for operation, patient clinical cardex, medicine cards, use of abbreviations, signatures and dates, preparation for theatre, consent forms		
Identification of patients		
Manuals, reference books, registers, reports (policy and procedure manuals, handing over reports, day and night reports, number and types of registers in place)		
Policies in place: staff development, overtime work, use of part-time staff		
Work schedules of staff (nursing, clerical, health-care workers, domestic)		
Patient safety		
Medico-legal risks, hazards, incidents, isolation procedures (fire and equipment)		
General appearance of the ward (hygienic status)		
Access given to relatives of seriously ill patients		

The following aspects are inspected and in order	✓	Needs attention
Monitoring nursing process		
Patient education programme		
Nursing procedures (intravenous therapy, psychosocial support)		
Multidisciplinary team approach (doctor rounds, paramedical staff)		
Dressing room		
Control (sterile packs and supplies, used needles and syringes, hand gloves)		
Cupboards (pharmaceutical supplies for external and internal use)		
Hygienic state of room		
Method of dealing with used dressing packs		
Blood transfusion control		
Control of blood containers, prescription, compatibility testing, fridge		
Administration procedure of blood (ordering, blood checking, storage of blood, blood books)		
Urine testing and facilities		
Control (content of locking cupboard, labelling, control of specimens)		
Teaching of staff		
Soiled linen		
Handling and control by staff		
Method of cleaning storage area		
Removal (route and place where it is handled, by whom)		
Policy on sluice room		
Cleaning and daily disinfection (wash-basins, mouth and sputum mugs, bedpans, urinals)		
Hygienic state of walls, floors		
Facilities for and control of infected linen and used items		
Cupboards for cleaning materials		
Daily cleaning (brooms, mops, other cleaning materials, dusters not feathers)		
Storage of these items		
Bathroom and toilets		
Hygienic state		
Bells		
State of floors (slippery)		
Stock room or facilities		
Hygienic state and ventilation		
Security measures (lock and key)		

The following aspects are inspected and in order	✓	Needs attention
Stock control (amount of stock, ordering and requisitioning process, checking)		
Procedure to obtain replacements		
Kitchen		
Hygienic state, e.g. basin, stove, fridge		
Condition of cutlery and crockery		
Control measures (what is kept in fridge, leftover food, control of supplies)		
Linen room		
Stock control and ordering process		
Hygienic state of room and linen		
Is policy of linen control being carried out?		
Ventilation of the room		
Light bulbs and safety, lock and key		
Interpersonal relationships		
Discipline and grievance procedures followed		
Communication: correspondence, memoranda writing		
Motivation and appearance of staff		
Methods used in decision-making, problem-solving, conflict management		
Method for improving productivity		
Doctor rounds and visiting system		
Patient complaints and client satisfaction monitoring		
Liaison interdepartmental		
Requesting laboratory specimens, X-ray tests		
Use of computers and maintenance		
Communication with top management		
Attendance meetings and in-service training sessions		
Quality control measures		
Control measures (method of safeguarding keys)		
Recordkeeping: Annual reports		
Relevant disaster plan in unit		
Handling of medico-legal incidents		
Cost management and control: budget preparations		
Improvement of work procedures		
Number of staff members versus patient load		
Research projects and implementation of research findings		

(Adapted from Jooste, 2001)

Answers to learning activities

Learning activity 1
Bookmark on supervision

This bookmark contains examples of reasons why a student nurse should be supervised.

BOOKMARK

> Top 10 reasons to supervise a student nurse
> 1 Develop and recruit future supervisees
> 2 Stay current, learn what students are learning
> 3 Develop your mentoring skills
> 4 Instil an image of a role model
> 5 Enhance clinical skills
> 6 Contribute to quality in the profession
> 7 Introduce student to the multidisciplinary approach
> 8 Encourage student to advocate for the service and profession
> 9 Promote networking with the educational component of training
> 10 Share your expertise.

Learning activity 2
Scenario

You could have mentioned the examples given below.

Protecting the welfare and best interest of the client
As sister in charge, she should accept the shared responsibility for client care.

Support to team members
The sister in charge could have experienced problems to manage her new job description, however, she still had to encourage her staff members to maintain professionalism, and not to label the patient as a difficult patient.

To provide the supervisee with a safe, protective relationship in which to be creative
A professional nurse should have been allocated on the left-side wing of the unit to assist with nursing care delivery. This could have promoted an opportunity for evaluation of the practice of the student nurses and would have encouraged students to maintain ethical and professional standards of practice and ensure accountability to the clients.

Monitoring the supervisee's performance and development
A professional nurse should have addressed the prevention of Mr X's bedsore timeously and should have monitored the professional practice of students in treating back and pressure parts. Record-keeping would then have been done correctly.

Improve own supervisory skills
The sister in charge needs to improve her instruction skills and capabilities, will have to develop decision-making skills on important priorities in the unit, and explore new possibilities to prevent medico-legal incidents. She will have to reflect on this incident.

Ensuring quality assurance in service delivery
The supervisor should have ensured effective and consistent service delivery by student nurses, through for example letting them give feedback on their care delivery and reading their recordings on Mr X.

Learning activity 3
Supervisory contract

Various examples of a supervisory contract document exist. In completing the contract, mention aspects of:
- Your job description
- Policies and priorities that need to be clarified
- The focus of the contract
- The method of supervision
- Any arrangements that need to be made to adhere to the contract.

Learning activity 4
Feedback on supervision of older people, friends and unions

Older people: Treat them as individuals, respect their skills, give them opportunities to take the lead, let them share their valuable information and knowledge, ask for their input

Friends: Talk about your role with them, agree to only talk about work at work

Unions: Know the union contracts and guidelines well, let an expert explain all the important labour issues for you

Learning activity 5
Role modelling

You have now determined the extent to which you are and should be a role model. One should be a good example in exercising good practice in a supervisory relationship. In this activity you completed a self-evaluation instrument in which you could determine in which aspects of role modelling you need to develop yourself as an effective supervisor.

Good supervisors really enjoy supervision, are committed to helping supervisees grow, and to prepare for and be involved in supervision sessions. These supervisors have a clear sense of their own strengths and limitations as a supervisor, and can identify how their personal traits and interpersonal style may affect the conduct of supervision. The personal trait of humour helps both the supervisor and supervisee get through rough spots in their work together and to achieve a healthy perspective on their work.

Learning activity 6
Motivational principles and examples

Motivational principles	Your examples
Understand the term 'motivation'	Motivation is a positive force to instil a good self-image opposed to fear. Read literature in nursing magazines on motivation.
Focus on job enrichment	Provide challenges in line with the skills of the supervisee. Make tasks more enjoyable. Focus on long-term gain of positive attitudes in a team.
Learn to like your supervisees	Focus on individuals and show an interest in them. Understand that each person is unique, every person has talents and strong points, acknowledge them. Get to know followers and their interests. Listen to what followers have to say. Take time to talk to supervisees. Recognise the contributions of supervisees. Promote a trusting relationship with supervisees.
Encourage participation in the unit	Involve supervisees in decisions where outcomes require their commitment. Provide opportunities for achievement through varied, interesting and challenging tasks or projects. Build interdependencies among supervisees that promote group cohesiveness. Encourage group projects.
Provide open communication in the unit	First-hand feedback on performances is essential. Let supervisees know how they are doing. Share new information with all supervisees regarding new policies or happenings, and prevent the grapevine.

Motivational principles	Your examples
Making work itself a motivator	Give supervisees more scope to vary the methods, sequence and pace of their tasks. Give supervisees the control information needed to monitor their own performances. Encourage participation in planning and evaluating new techniques and skills. Increase individual responsibility for achieving defined targets or standards. Create a friendly environment in the unit that is free from the use of bad gestures and language.
Lead the way by example	Act energetically and strive to reach new heights of energy. Always be neat on oneself and wear the necessary devices as expected from SANC regulations.
Reward accomplishments	Set targets that require a little extra effort. Inform supervisees about what they have to do to gain the rewards they seek. Place the responsibilities with the supervisee. Give praise when praise is due. Praise publicly.
Instil a desire to achieve goals	Exploit the benefits from competition carefully. Set measurable outcomes and rewards to motivate supervisees to obtain them, create fun activities.
Provide opportunities for growth in the unit	Motivate supervisees by revealing the opportunities in the organisation for taking on additional responsibilities, for resolving problems, for sharing, for recognition, for achievement. Give all supervisees the opportunity to attend an in-service training session or workshop in which they may also be the presenter.

Learning activity 7
Skills in supervision

The supervisor should possess certain skills in supervision. Some of these are:

Be available when needed. Nurse managers should schedule regular meetings and make themselves available for urgent matters.

Supervisors should praise when necessary. Compliments do not take too much time, and a quick short note to a staff member can make a difference.

With a heavy managerial load, supervisors may find it difficult to remain abreast of day-to-day issues in the work environment. Schedule at least a few hours a week with the team to increase your credibility as a supervisor.

Supervisors should determine their ability to make decisions or the reason for procrastination. Staff members should know where the responsibilities of the supervisor in decisions begin and end. On certain occasions it is better to first have sufficient time to think about a decision, before announcing it. A supervisor is expected to make timely decisions based on the availability of evidence and information.

A supervisor should listen attentively and patiently, which requires making an effort.

Favouratism will lead to low staff morale. It is proper to assign a task to a supervisee who is better equipped than others to manage; however, it is improper to delegate important tasks more often to a supervisee who is popular, or to deny others the opportunity to develop their talents and skills.

Learning activity 8
Characteristics of a supervisor

Research has shown that the average supervisor:
- Is between 31 and 50 years old
- Has been in the specific institution for 5 to 15 years
- Has less than 5 years of supervisory experience
- Has a high-school education
- A minority of supervisors have a university qualification.

Learning activity 9
Quality assurance measures

Your activity is completed. In this activity you should have realised the extent of the aspects to be monitored in the unit in order to be in line with the policies and procedures of the service. This is your quality assurance tool to stay focused on the vision of rendering a quality service.

Learning activity 10
Weaknesses in the unit

Below is an example of a feedback plan to address weaknesses in the unit

Shortcomings in Ward B	Objectives	Actions	Person responsible	Due date
Absenteeism	To promote effective use of human resources	Evaluate the current duty roster and schedules worked. View the complaint and request book of staff members. Follow up on reasons for absenteeism. Follow the disciplinary procedure.	Sr Mogobe	1 month

Shortcomings in Ward B	Objectives	Actions	Person responsible	Due date
Poor recording of used supplies	Cost-effectiveness in the utilisation of supplies	Provide in-service training sessions on the budget. Include the topic of recordkeeping and cost-effectiveness in orientation sessions. Show price list of supplies.	**Sr Allen**	1 month
Policy on overtime not followed	To implement policies effectively	Review the authorisation process. Give written warnings.	**Supervisor**	Immediately
Feedback of patients is not always made known	To address the problems clients experience in the unit	Plan in-service on importance of feedback, patient rights. Ensure anonymity of participants.	**Sr Allen**	1 week
Conflicts in the unit are badly managed	To promote interpersonal relationships in the unit	Review allocation of staff members. Hold climate meeting. Follow principles of conflict management. Use a reward system	**Supervisor**	1 month
Staff members do not attend scheduled sessions	To encourage staff development of staff members	Outline the legal details of the Skills Development Act. Make attendance of staff development sessions a requirement for promotion.	**Supervisor**	1 month

Learning activity 11
Combating negligence in the unit

You have completed the activity and should note the importance of this instrument to combat negligence in your unit.

Learning activity 12
Professional behaviour

The enrolled midwife (staff nurse level) fell under the supervision of a professional midwife, who at no stage showed involvement in the case. The enrolled midwife did not establish and maintain, in the execution of the midwifery regimen, an environment in which the physical and mental health of mother and child were promoted.

Enrolled staff and professional midwives should have the necessary knowledge, skills, values and attitudes expected in midwifery practice and should, along with their authority and the responsibility they had accepted to care for the mother and child, be accountable for their own acts and omissions.

The enrolled midwife was responsible for this mother and baby because she completed the partogram and progress report. She was still under the supervision of a professional midwife.

The professional midwife had, among others, some of the following responsibilities:

- She should have kept clear and accurate records of the progress of labour and all acts that were performed in connection with the mother and child.
- She should have monitored the vital signs of the mother and baby.
- She should have monitored, recorded and reported the reaction of the mother and child to medication and treatment. The nausea of the mother that started should have been reported to the doctor, along with the reason for starting the Syntocinon drip.
- She should have avoided the delay in obtaining medical assistance.
- Facilitation of communication with the mother in the execution of the midwifery regimen was required.

Learning activity 13
Evaluating own shortcomings

You have completed an instrument to evaluate your own shortcomings. Now that you are aware of them, take one aspect at a time and work on it. By doing this you will create a more positive work environment for the whole unit, because you are the leader and role model.

Learning activity 14
Staff development role

You have done your last activity, and in this activity you also used your staff development function to guide a novice student. Evaluate all the aspects that need attention, and explain to the student why it is necessary to pay attention to these aspects to avoid medico-legal risks, negligence to the patient and an adequate environment to staff members to provide an efficient service.

Case studies

Case Study 1: Conceptualisation of supervision

Staff Nurse Birdy was on night duty on the 3rd of August in Ward P, working under the supervision of Chief Professional Nurse Mello, the night supervisor. Her co-workers were Staff Nurse Motiba and a security guard. There were 19 patients in the unit, including Mr Zulu Gumbi.

According to Nurse Birdy, Mr Gumbi became restless at 22h00 and was disturbing the other patients. Nurse Birdy decided to take the patient to a seclusion area and to observe him two-hourly. According to Nurse Birdy she tried, without success, to contact Nurse Mello to inform him about this intervention. Nurse Birdy also claimed that she could not take the patient's vital signs due to the patient's restlessness.

Nurse Motiba was on duty the same night under the supervision of Nurse Birdy. He followed Nurse Birdy's instructions and thought he had no right to question her when she requested that he assist with moving Mr Gumbi. Dr Guba, the doctor looking after Mr Gumbi, was not informed about the decision to put the patient in seclusion.

At 04h20 on the 4th of August, the patient, Mr Zulu Gumbi, was found dead by Nurse Motiba. Nurse Motiba stated that he had found the patient naked on a bare mattress with only two thin blankets. The patient was in a kneeling position. The room had high ceilings and no windows.

Nurse Birdy informed both Dr Guba and Nurse Mello about the death of Mr Gumbi. Dr Guba said she had not been called about the change in the patient's condition and had only been called when she was requested to come and certify the death of the patient.

Mrs Katharina Louw, the Nursing Service Manager, was asked to investigate the incident. During the investigation, it was found that Nurse Mello, as the night supervisor on the said night, was indirectly overseeing Ward P, as there were no professional nurses allocated to that ward. No recordings of the incident were found on the patient's records. Nurse Mello stated that he had not been called when the condition of the said patient had changed and was only called by Nurse Birdy when the patient had been found dead. When Nurse Mello arrived in Ward P, he found the patient in the seclusion room, naked and in a kneeling position on a mattress.

The hospital had a seclusion protocol that the two staff nurses were aware of.

- Mr Gumbi was placed in a seclusion room, which had not been prescribed by the doctor.
- Nurses Birdy and Motiba failed to report the incident to the night supervisor when the said patient's condition changed.
- Both nurses failed to continuously monitor any vital signs even though the condition of the said patient warranted such monitoring.
- The nurses failed to protect the patient against accidents, injuries and other trauma.
- Both nurses failed to provide the patient with adequate and effective patient advocacy.
- Both nurses failed to promote and maintain the necessary hygiene, physical comfort and reassurance that the said patient required.
- Finally, the nurses negligently failed to keep clear and accurate records of all acts performed in connection with the said patient.

Questions

Read through Chapter 1 in order to understand the concept of supervision.
1   The term 'supervisor' typically refers to one's immediate superior in the workplace, that is, the person to whom you directly report. Supervision is the activity carried out by supervisors to oversee the performance or productivity and progress of their supervisees. In the scenario above, a focus is placed on an incident that happened in Ward P and not on the role of the supervisor Nurse Mello.
    1.1   How do you view the role of Nurse Mello in this scenario?
    1.2   How should Nurse Mello have ensured that the nurses conformed to the policies and other internal regulations in the nursing service?
2   What were the legal and professional responsibilities of Staff Nurses Birdy and Motiba regarding their scope of practice?
3   What tips would you provide to supervisors regarding the supervision of supervisees?
4   What are the lessons learned from this scenario? Focus on both the roles of supervisors and the supervisees.

Conclusion

Policies and guidelines are set to assist nursing staff with how to act in specific situations, as well as to protect them. If the said protocol had been followed, this unfortunate incident would not have happened. Nurses are entrusted with the health of patients under their care, and nursing regulations such as the scope of practice are there to guide and assist nurses on what is expected of them. There is a relationship contract that exists between the profession and the community and this relationship is based on trust. This incident had not only compromised this true relationship but also brought the profession into disrepute. Nurses have a responsibility towards the safety of patients physically, emotionally and psychologically, more so when patients are vulnerable, such as psychiatric patients. There is and never will be any justification for nurses not caring about their patients.

When nurses accept the responsibility to care for or to nurse a patient, they accept total responsibility for the patient, as well as for their own acts and omissions. By accepting responsibility for the care of patients, nurses are also required by law to keep accurate records of all their actions, irrespective of their category. Nurses should ensure that they are continuously undergoing staff development in professional practice and unit management, specifically also in effective clinical supervision of the delivery of patient care.

Case study 2: The role of a supervisor during verbal abuse among colleagues

Professional Nurse Mosonto was in charge of Ward K in an academic hospital and was the supervisor of Nurse Sebantu and Staff Nurse Rasinga. Also involved in this case is Professional Nurse Sibia, who was second in charge in the Casualty Ward.

Around 10h00 in the morning, Nurse Sebantu left Ward K and went to the Casualty Ward. Nurse Sebantu made quite a lot of noise as she looked for one of her friends, Nurse Moloi. This noise disturbed consultations. Nurse Sibia requested Nurse Sebantu to go to Nurse Moloi quietly instead of calling her name loudly. With that, Nurse Sebantu started swearing at him, saying that he had made a pass at her and that he was as ugly as his kids. Nurse Sebantu then left the Casualty Ward to return to Ward K.

Nurse Rasinga also worked in Ward K and saw Nurse Sebantu when she returned to Ward K. She later also saw Nurse Sibia talking to Nurses Mosonto and Sebantu. Nurse Rasinga asked Nurse Sebantu what was happening – Nurse Sebantu indicated that Nurse Sibia was giving her trouble – she claimed he had made a pass at her.

Nurse Sibia decided to go to Ward K. He went to his colleague in charge of Casualty, and told him that he was going to Ward K but he did not tell him why he was going there.

Upon arrival in Ward K he met Nurse Sebantu and stated that he was going to report the incident to Nurse Mosonto. He claims that Nurse Sebantu continued to shout and swear at him. Nurse Sibia reported the incident to Nurse Mosonto, who spoke to both of them and tried to intervene to settle the dispute. Nurse Mosonto then left for the tearoom.

However, Nurse Sebantu continued to shout at Nurse Sibia and he claims that as he left Ward K, he heard Nurse Sebantu calling him 'rubbish', after which he turned back and approached her. Nurse Sibia asked Nurse Sebantu to stop shouting and swearing at him, but she continued. Nurse Sibia then tried to strangle Nurse Sebantu.

Nurse Mosonto came back from the tearoom to speak to the two of them. She found Nurse Sebantu crying and making quite a bit of noise. Nurse Sibia was loudly telling Nurse Sebantu 'never to say that to me again'. Nurse Sebantu told Nurse Mosonto that Nurse Sibia had tried to strangle her. Nurse Mosonto tried once more to intervene, however, Nurse Sebantu told her that she was going to the police to lay a charge of assault. With that she left.

Nurse Rasinga saw everything as it was happening, and also saw that Nurse Sebantu was crying after Nurse Sibia had tried to strangle her. Some of the patients in Ward K were watching the event.

- Nurse Sebantu wrongfully and verbally abused a collegue, Nurse Sibia, whilst he was providing nursing care to his patients. She also wrongfully abandoned patients who were under her care in Ward K when she verbally abused Nurse Sibia.
- Nurse Sibia wrongfully assaulted a colleague, namely Nurse Sebantu, while on duty and wrongfully abandoned patients who were under his care in the Casualty Ward when he engaged in a shouting match with the said colleague.

Questions

1 The **roles** of a supervisor could include acting as a coach, consultant, mentor, role model, advocate, counsellor, and motivator in nursing practice. How could Professional Nurse Mosonto have used these roles more effectively in this situation?
2 How did Professional Nurse Mosonto monitor and supervise the situation?
3 Group supervision has certain strengths and potential challenges. Comment on the following possibilities:

Strengths	Potential challenges
Input is received from a number of people.	Individual needs may not be addressed.
A supportive atmosphere exists among peers.	Individuals may get 'lost' or 'hide' within the group.
There is the value of listening to others describe their work and problems they face.	There may be a lack of time for group members with large caseloads.
It is cost effective in terms of time and economics.	Not all are suited to group work.
It allows for experimentation with other interventions.	It can be used as a 'dumping ground'.
It can help supervisees deal with issues of dependency on supervisors.	Group dynamics may temporarily block the task at hand.
There is evaluation and feedback from a number of people.	There is pressure to conform, eg 'Group think'.
Risk taking can be higher in a group setting.	Newcomers may find it difficult to enter a group.
There is emotional support from peers.	Some topics may not be of interest to other group members.
Issues arising from within the group can be addressed.	There may be lessening of confidentiality.
It dilutes the power of supervisors.	It may mean an overload for some members.

Conclusion

A nurse has a two-fold responsibility, namely to the patient and to the profession, in upholding the image of the profession and the relevant ethical responsibilities. When any patient enters the health service, he or she has the right to be cared for in a safe environment that is conducive to the healing process. This safe environment refers to the holistic care and supervision that a patient is entitled to, which includes caring for the patient, and ensuring the physical and psychosocial wellbeing of the patient.

When a nurse accepts this responsibility he or she has to ensure that nursing care of a high standard is rendered where the members of the community will feel safe regarding all aspects of care. One cannot blame patients or colleagues if they are of the opinion that the image of the nursing profession was tarnished and that they might not feel safe in such an environment.

Incidents like the one above act as warning signs to nurses to always reflect on their actions at all times to ensure supervision of professional behaviour in all fields of nursing practice. Only by doing that and acting in a disciplined and professional way can nurses retain the respect of the community.

Case study 3: Supervision of progress in labour

A patient, Mrs Albie Neelt, went to the hospital one morning because she was in labour. On admission she was assessed by Midwife Aldie Moore.

On examination it was found that Mrs Neelt was in her 38th week of gestation and in advanced labour. Midwife Moore listened to the fetal heart rate and told Mrs Neelt that she was in labour and would deliver very soon. She then left to do her four-hourly rounds as she was responsible for the entire maternity unit, which included the Antenatal, Labour, Postnatal and Neonatal Wards.

Mrs Neelt was then admitted to a private room and left on her own. Her husband wanted to stay until after the delivery, but was sent home by Midwife Moore. When Midwife Moore left the admission room, she told Mrs Neelt to call her when she needed assistance. Shortly thereafter Mrs Neelt started to experience severe contractions. Mrs Neelt could see Midwife Moore outside her room but Midwife Moore did not come and attend to her. The contractions became worse and Mrs Neelt shouted for help but nobody came to her assistance. She then delivered on her own. When Midwife Moore entered the private room she was angry with Mrs Neelt for delivering on her own and wanted to know why Mrs Neelt had not called her.

Midwife Moore took the baby and wrapped him. The mother wanted to hold her baby but her request was refused. Mrs Neelt asked Midwife Moore where she was taking the baby and was told that she was taking the baby to be bathed. The next morning when her husband came to visit he wanted to know where the baby was. Mrs Neelt told him that they had taken the baby to another room to be bathed the previous day, and that she had not been given the opportunity to hold her baby. The husband inquired from nurses where the baby was and was referred to the nursery. When he looked at his child he saw that baby's arm was in plaster. No explanation could be given to him. He requested to see Midwife Moore but was told that she was off duty.

After realising that nobody could account for the baby's broken arm, he requested that his wife and the baby be discharged. Mrs Neelt was given a document to sign by the day nurse who was unknown to her. When she asked why she had to sign the document she was informed that it served as proof that she had been a patient in the hospital. She then left the hospital with her husband.

On investigation by the Nursing Service Manager, Mrs Carstens (a midwife with many years experience), the hospital records indicated that the assessment and examination done to Mrs Neelt from admission and throughout the labour process had been substandard.

Risk factors had not been identified and managed properly, gestational age and fetal condition were not accurately recorded, the outcomes of the pregnancy, which are essential for every woman who presents herself for care, were not clearly reflected. The records reflected conflicting information, which was misleading, inaccurate and incomplete. On the day Mrs Neelt had been admitted, the ward had not been abnormally busy.

During the investigation, Midwife Moore stated that she had an overload of work because she was responsible for the whole maternity unit without the support of her two colleagues. She said she had to do four-hourly rounds in the Antenatal Ward, she had to attend to a fresh caesarean section patient and assist mothers putting their babies to the breast. She stated that she had not been able to arrive in time to manage Mrs Neelt's delivery.

The investigation also indicated that the inscriptions in Mrs Neelt's records had been tampered with. The records indicated a healthy fetus, that it was in the correct position, and could be delivered without complications. Midwife Moore admitted that she was the one who had done the overwriting and she confessed that she had confused Mrs Neelt's records with those of another patient.

Midwife Moore:
- negligently failed to accurately assess, examine and continuously monitor a patient who was in labour,
- failed to continuously monitor the fetal condition,
- abandoned a patient in labour, which resulted in an unattended delivery of the said patient's baby,
- failed to provide an accurate record of the outcome of the delivery of the baby of the said patient,
- failed to identify the baby's broken arm and report it to the mother,
- failed to keep clear and accurate records of the said patient.

Questionnaire

On the questionnaire overleaf, evaluate to what extent Midwife Moore was effective in her clinical supervision of Mrs Neelt.

KEY: 1 = no extent 2 = small extent 3 = moderate extent 4 = full extent	1	2	3	4
Practise within the ethical framework of the nursing profession				
Followed the ethical principles and the professional code of ethics in delivering healthcare service				
Practised the principles of scientifically based nursing care				
Ensured safe storage of patients' valuables				
Nursing process				
Identified patients through the correct procedure				
Implemented nursing methods and procedures allocated to them correctly				
Promote multi-professional and multi-disciplinary teamwork and networking in the interest of patient care				
Appropriately referred patients to other members of the health team				
Performed nursing assessments adequately in terms of risk assessment and mental state examinations of patients				
Liaised with the doctor regarding discharge planning				
Patient and family involvement				
Gathered information from relatives/carers who accompanied patients to hospital				
Maintained a constant safe environment for patients based on their risk assessment				
Patient education				
Orientated patients towards the Ward environment and daily routine				
Ensured that patients were provided with written statements of their 'rights and responsibilities'				
Provided an explanation of and ensurde patients' understanding of rights and responsibilities				
Planning of patient care				
Ensured that patients were aware of, understood and were involved in their treatment plan				
Ensured that treatments and procedures were completed, i.e. X-rays, blood specimens, preparation for theatre				
Implementation of the nursing plan				
Delivered comprehensive nursing care to patients within the practice setting				
Administered prescribed medication correctly				
Provided ongoing monitoring and reporting of patients' mental and physical health status				
Monitored the observations of patients timeously				

Completed the daily score card of the health status of patients				
Needed direction and supervision in the care of their patients				
Provided education and counselling towards the promotion of the health status improvement of patients within the practice setting				
Evaluate nursing care				
Nursing staff summarised the decisions made in the ward round and documented the nursing care plan as soon as possible after the ward round				
Completed the necessary discharge records				
Ensured that appropriate plans were in place to facilitate patients' return to their community				

Conclusion

A major responsibility in clinical supervision is to prevent negligence in patient care. There should be a balance between the rights of the public and the rights of the nurse with the protection of the public at heart. In this particular case a young mother entrusted the life of herself and her unborn baby to the care of the professional midwife. This incident leads to a total breakdown in the trust relationship between a vulnerable patient and a midwife.

Case study 4: Supervision of competencies of supervisees

Mrs Kay Ransi was admitted to hospital and underwent an operation. Professional Nurse Zebo and Staff Nuse Nantz worked on the ward where Mrs Ransi returned after her operation. Dr Malato was the doctor in charge.

After the operation when she was back in the ward Mrs Ransi started vomiting. Dr Malato ordered the insertion of a nasogastric tube. Nurse Zebo was working in the general ward on the said date and was given the instruction by Dr Malato to pass a nasogastric tube on Mrs Ransi. Mrs Ransi asked the doctor not to insert the tube until after visiting hours as it would upset her family – they would think that she was very ill. The doctor agreed. In the meantime, Nurse Nantz was instructed by Nurse Zebo to carry out the procedure. When Nurse Nantz went to Mrs Ransi the patient repeated her request to do it later as she did not want to alarm her children. After visiting hours, Nurse Zebo again sent Nurse Nantz to insert the tube. Nurse Nantz spoke harshly to the patient, who was at that stage vomiting while the tube was being inserted. Nurse Nantz was in a hurry because she did not want to leave the task for the night staff. The nasogastric tube was inserted incorrectly by Nurse Nantz and the patient was injured.

The patient's daughter, Ms Lydia Sams went to the hospital on the said day and found her mother covered in vomit and blood, lying in the bed naked and covered only with a hospital robe. Mrs Ransi was holding the tube with her arm supported on a pillow. Nurse Nantz told Ms Sams that her mother 'keeps dying and waking up'.

Staff Nurse Nantz:
* abused the patient verbally
* performed a procedure incorrectly
* failed to make the patient comfortable and provide basic nursing care after the insertion of the nasogastric tube
* failed to report to a professional nurse that the patient was vomiting
* failed to keep clear and accurate records.

Questions

Should Nurse Zebo have:
1 ensured that Nurse Nantz inserted the nasogastric tube correctly?
2 analysed the task to identify and evaluate the hazards in terms of safety measures (training)?
3 evaluated whether Nurse Nantz was qualified to perform the job, and whether she knew how to perform the job? Had requirements for training been determined?
4 scheduled, co-ordinated, directed and discussed all aspects of the task while providing details?
5 evaluated Nurse Nantz's performance by observation and through communication with her supervisee and the patient?
6 adjusted (where necessary) the procedure for future nasogastric tube insertion?
7 made sure that steps were in place to evaluate the overall performance of Nurse Nantz over time?
8 set performance standards for supervisees (ensured quantifiable objectives), evaluated their behaviour, discussed performance indicators with supervisees (strengths, weaknesses, improvement needed), and initiated disciplinary measures?

Give reasons for your answers.

Conclusion

Supervision is the term used to describe planned regular periods of time that a supervisor monitors the supervisee's work and learning progress. Supervision is a multi-dimensional process which should provide the following functions:
* Evaluation of the performance of supervisees
* Monitoring levels and priorities of workload.

Supervision should provide a forum to assess the nurse–patient relationship and professional development. It should be supportive and motivational, educative and modelling. Clinical supervision looks at the nurse's behaviour within the nurse–patient relationship.

Case study 5: Abuse under supervision

Mr Bobo was matron of a psychiatric unit. Professional Nurse Motto was the direct supervisor of Professional Nurse Heath. Nurse Motto reported to Mr Bobo that patient Xaba Masiti had been beaten by Nurse Heath. Staff Nurses Litilio and Baloi worked on the same ward. Mr Bobo was informed that Nurse Heath was absent on sick leave because he had a bruised eye.

Nurse Heath went to Mr Bobo's home whilst on sick leave asking for advice, and confessed to assaulting the patient, stating that he had been scared.

Nurse Heath was second in charge of the ward. On the day in question, he met the patient on his way to the bathroom. He asked the patient why he was not under supervision and not with the other patients, upon which the patient hit Nurse Heath with a fist on his left eye. Nurse Heath slapped the patient in the face; the patient lost balance and fell. Nurse Heath continued to slap the patient on the chest and abdomen.

Nurse Baloi was working in the unit at the time of the incident. He was on duty and busy kitting the clothes for a new patient admission, when he heard a patient screaming from the left side wing of the ward. He went out and saw Nurse Heath assaulting the patient – the patient was not fighting back. Nurse Heath was sitting on the patient and hitting him continuously on the head.

Nurse Heath then dragged the patient to the seclusion room and bashed the patient's head against the wall, at least twice. Nurse Baloi did not know what the reason for the assault was and assisted Nurse Heath in holding the patient down. Nurse Heath then went to fetch an injection to give to the patient in the seclusion room. During this time the patient kept on asking what he had done wrong to be assaulted so badly. Nurse Baloi saw the swelling on the patient's face and eyes, as well as patches where hair had been pulled out. He didn't see a doctor treating this patient or checking for injuries after the incident.

Nurse Litilio wanted to go to lunch but a new patient arrived and she was busy with the admission. She heard a patient screaming for help from another room, calling out 'why are you hitting me?' She peeped into the room and saw Nurse Heath and the patient holding one another and Nurse Heath hitting the patient. She ran up to them and separated them. Nurse Heath continued hitting the patient while Nurse Baloi held the patient down. Nurse Baloi then released the patient, and the patient, together with Nurse Heath ended up struggling and landed on the floor. Nurse Heath was on top of the patient and continued to assault the patient with his fists. The patient screamed for Nurse Heath to stop but he didn't.

The patient was pulled by the hair into the seclusion room by Nurse Heath. This was done without the doctor's prescription. In the seclusion room the patient was hit against the wall. Nurse Health left to fetch an injection. During that time the patient was crying and asked what he had done wrong. The patient was held down and an injection given. Nurse Heath drew blood specimens from the patient.

The next day the patient had a swollen face and a blue eye because of this incident.

This whole incident was witnessed by Nurse Motto, who was in charge and did not intervene in the incident.

Professional Nurse Heath:
- willfully and physically assaulted a patient who was under his care
- acted beyond his scope of practice when he prescribed the seclusion room for the said patient
- failed to promptly summon the medical practitioner to examine the extent of the injuries on the said patient
- failed to provide adequate and effective patient advocacy for the said patient
- failed to keep clear and accurate records of all actions performed in connection with the said patient.

Questions

1 With regard to Professional Nurse Motto (who witnessed the whole incident without intervention) what role should he have played?
2 What do you perceive as weaknesses in supervisory actions in this scenario?
3 Which aspects should be addressed in policy documents that could address prevention of a similar incident, and that relate to human resources management, staffing, development, interpersonal relationships?
4 How should a professional nurse in charge of a unit supervise and monitor the behaviour of staff?
5 Interpersonal process recall is a model particularly suited to self-supervision. Imagine you are in Professional Nurse Heath's position and answer the following questions:
   5.1 What would you feel?
   5.2 What would you think?
   5.3 What bodily sensations would you have?
   5.4 What would you do or say?
   5.5 What would you rather have done or said?
   5.6 What would the risks be if you had done/said this?
   5.7 What do you imagine this person was thinking/feeling?
   5.8 What images, associations, memories does this bring up?
   5.9 Anything else?

Modified by Vicki Yarker-Hitchcock 2004 from 'Introduction to clinical/professional' on http://www.clinical-supervision.com/.

Conclusion

In terms of the legislation governing the profession of nursing, i.e. the Nursing Act, the Batho Pele policy document, the Mental Health Act, the ethics of the profession, the Patients' Rights Charter and many others, under no circumstances is a nurse allowed to hit a patient, no matter what. During the fight the patient fell, which in itself warranted that the doctor be called to assess his condition, but this was not done. This happened while Nurse Motto was acting as the direct supervisor of Nurse Heath.

There is a relationship that exists between the community and the nursing profession, and this relationship is based on trust. Nurses are entrusted with the responsibility to give due care and adequate supervision, especially if the patient is vulnerable, such as a psychiatric patient.

There is and shall never be any justification for nurses to abuse patients verbally, psychologically or physically as was the case here. The practice of nurses is regulated by legislation known by all nurses and there is no excuse for transgressing the laws, whether by action or omission. This unethical behaviour compromised the trust relationship that exists between the profession and the community.

Case study 6: Supervision of scheduled medicine

Ms Gugu Sebela was a Nursing Service Manager at a healthcare centre. Ms Sebela discovered that there was a discrepancy in the records of scheduled medicine – ten ampules of Valium 10 mg were unaccounted for. Professional Nurse Freda Mouton had signed in the drug register that she had received the Valium ampoules but then later claimed that in fact these drugs were never delivered.

Nurse Mouton was on duty in Ward K on the day in question and was the person who received medicines. The driver who brought the medicines was in such a hurry that she did not have time to check the stock and she simply signed without checking. She discovered later that the Valium ampoules had in fact not been delivered – the box that should have contained the Valium was the incorrect box and it had to be returned to the drug company – she had signed the invoice assuming that the box contained Valium. She was found guilty during an internal disciplinary hearing.

Professional Nurse Mouton:
* failed as a supervisor in ensuring the safekeeping of scheduled medication.

Questions
What quality control measures should be taken regarding the following:
1   Control measures (method of safeguarding keys)?
2   Record keeping of scheduled drugs?
3   Receiving of scheduled drugs?
4   Counting of scheduled drugs?
5   Handling of medico-legal incidents regarding drugs?
6   Cost management and control of drugs?
7   Improvement of work procedures of managing drugs?

Conclusion

Part of the role of a professional nurse is supervision of scheduled medicines. Specific procedures and control measures must be followed. Professional Nurse Freda Mouton did not follow the correct procedures in the supervision of scheduled drugs. Nurses are taught and licensed accordingly and must always exercise caution when dealing with drugs with regard to ordering, safe keeping and control.

Case study 7: Supervision in the labour ward

The patient, Mrs Sila Foster, was referred by Dr Nico Bengu after she was examined and an ultra-sonography had been done. She was admitted to the maternity ward at the general hospital with a diagnosis of being in labour.

On arrival at the hospital she was seen by a doctor who performed a vaginal examination. It was found that she was 1 cm dilated, with no contractions and the doctor concluded that she was not in labour. She was therefore discharged and told to come back when she was in labour.

She then insisted on being admitted because she lived far from the hospital and would have problems with transport if she went into labour at night.

She was then admitted to the lying-in-ward with a doctor's instruction that contractions should be monitored. She was taken from the maternity ward to the lying-in-ward by a nurse who handed her over to Midwife Masinga with a report that she had insisted on being admitted, despite the fact that she was told that she was not in labour.

Midwife Masinga asked her why she was resisting going home and whether she liked being in hospital; Mrs Foster explained that she was the only adult at home and it would be difficult to come back during the night. She was then shown a bed by Midwife Masinga. Later on, Mrs Foster was called from her bed to answer administrative questions and explain where she was working. She was also asked why she didn't deliver at another clinic, upon which she responded that she did not have medical aid and therefore could not afford medical costs. She was then told to go back to bed, where she experienced pain on an on-and-off basis. Mrs Foster mentioned the pains to Midwife Masinga, who ignored her complaint.

When the night staff came on duty Midwife Masinga handed Mrs Foster over to them, telling them that Mrs Foster had insisted on being admitted and refused to go home.

Early in the evening Mrs Foster experienced strong contractions. She went to the nurses to ask for help but was told that she was not in labour and would only deliver in two weeks. She walked up and down and tried to resist the pain.

After the night staff had given the other patients their medication, they went and sat in the baby room, with their legs on chairs, covered with hospital sheets, and put the lights off in the baby room.

Early the next morning Mrs Foster's membranes ruptured and she went and knocked on the door of the baby room where the nurses were. The nurses then said to her: 'Is it you again?' She told them that her membrane had ruptured and they told her that she was boring them as all they were interested in was the baby's head. Mrs Foster then stood there, hoping they would sympathise and attend to her.

While standing there she noticed that her waters were mixed with blood. She reported this to the night staff and was told she could remain standing there. She stood there until the day staff came in, when she grabbed a professional nurse and asked for help. The sister then took her to the labour ward and handed her over to Midwife Makau in the labour ward.

Mrs Foster went into established labour unmonitored.

Midwife Makau examined her and called the doctor. She was then taken to the theatre for a caesarean section, after which she was told that her baby had died.

The Nursing Act and Regulations of the profession clearly state that if you accept responsibility, you inevitably also accept accountability. The scope of practice for midwives clearly stipulates what is expected of a midwife.

The midwives on night duty did not supervise:
- the monitoring of the vital signs of the mother and the baby
- that a safe environment was created for patients in the maternity and/or lying-in ward
- the progress of the patient's labour process
- the patient through adequate interpersonal relationships
- a patient in need of midwifery care
- within their legal and professional framework.

Questions

1 What are the most important reasons for supervising a women in labour?
2 Which supervisory skills were absent among the night staff?
3 Which actions should be taken to monitor the supervision of patients in a maternity ward?

Conclusion

Professional midwives enter the nursing profession by choice. Since nursing is a scientific profession, it implies that its practitioners should at all times be adequately skilled and trained to deliver the basic nursing and midwifery care necessary to patients. Midwives should supervise a women in labour, and be able to determine scientifically what the actual condition of a patient in labour is, and not merely look at the patient's facial expressions to see if she is in pain or wait for the patient to come forward with a complaint.

Patients come to hospital because they trust that nurses will supervise their labour process and are skilled to undertake their observations. It is the duty of every nurse practitioner to ensure that he or she is up-to-date with basic nursing care practices and in accepting his or her delegated task. If not, as independent practitioners they have an obligation to voice their concerns as expected from a professional person.

Inadequate resources, workforce and material should never be used as justification for not supervising patients. This is the vicarious liability of the employer as well as to ensure that a safe environment is created for nurses to deliver adequate nursing care. In the absence of a doctor, the professional midwife acts as the employer and carries this responsibility.

The golden rule that says 'if it is not recorded in the patient's record, then it has not been done' is a worldwide principle in the nursing profession and is as old as the profession itself.

Case study 8: Supervision of supervisees

Mr Petrus Dikeledi was the Chief Professional Nurse in an ICU. He was an experienced professional with 22 years of experience. One afternoon Staff Nurse Morris came to him and reported that an incident had occurred in her cubicle. This is what occurred:

Earlier that day, Nurse Dikeledi had phoned Dr Frik Freud, who was in charge of the patient in question (Mr Jaku). Dr Freud gave telephonic instructions that the patient be given pain medicine intra-arterially. Nurse Dikeledi gave instructions to Nurse Morris for the medication to be administered.

Sometime later, Nurse Dikeledi realised that the medication had not had an effect on the patient and he again called Dr Freud, who ordered pain medication to be given again.

Nurse Morris was allocated to the patient (Mr Jaku) by Nurse Dikeledi. On checking the intravenous vacoliters and the oxygen flow meters in the ICU, Nurse Morris discovered that Student Nurse Sims had given the second injection through the wrong route, i.e. through the arterial line.

Nurse Morris immediately reported the incident to Mr Dikeledi. Nurse Morris claimed that she did not hear Student Nurse Sims enter the cubicle nor see her. She felt that she was not responsible for the supervision of the student. She admitted that she was in the same cubicle with the student nurse at the time of the incident.

The patient nearly lost his arm as a result of the administration of the injection.

- Mr Dikeledi failed to appropriately and effectively provide adequate supervision to his subordinates after delegating them to render care to the patient.
- Nurse Morris failed to give clear and accurate instructions to Student Nurse Sims.
- There was no clear communication between Nurse Morris and Student Nurse Sims, which compromised the health of the patient.

Questions

Answer the following questions using a simple reflective model:

1   *Description*: What happened in this scenario? Tell the story in your own words.
2   *Feeling*: After telling this story, what are you thinking and feeling?
3   *Evaluation*: What was good and bad about the scenario?
4   *Analysis*: What sense can you make of the situation? Think about what this means to you.
5   *Conclusion*: What else could Mr Petrus Dikeledi have done and why did he not do that?
6   *Action plan*: If a similiar situation arose again, what should be done?
7   Is it a situation one can expect to deal with again?

(Modified by Vicki Yarker-Hitchcock 2004 from 'Introduction to clinical/professional' on http://www.clinical-supervision.com/).

Conclusion

Supervision means different things at different stages of our development as practitioners and the amount of supervision required in a clinical setting varies. In an ICU setting, more supervision is needed than in a clinic setting, as a result of the acute illnesses treated. Supervision is a very personal thing and unless supervisors attend formal training, supervision provided by them is likely to be based on their experience rather than on sound principles. Nurse Dikeledi had been working in an ICU setting for 22 years. Supervision is the activity carried out by supervisors to oversee the performance or productivity and progress of their supervisees who report directly to them.

Arrangement for supervision should be agreed between supervisor and supervisees, and formalised in either verbal or written contracts, covering job descriptions, policies and priorities, supervisor's expectations, supervisees' expectations and team expectations.

Certain specific skills are required by an ICU supervisor:

- Communication skills: To listen attentively and actively and to be able to comment openly, objectively and constructively.
- Supportive skills: To be able to identify when support is needed and offer supportive responses.
- Specialist skills: Nurses who specialise in particular therapies or fields of work should have access to supervision by someone who is similarly oriented.

Case study 9: Client supervision

Mr Jacob Teels went to a clinic because of a distended abdomen and swollen feet. He complained of constipation and intestinal problems. He was seen by Professional Nurse Danielle Richter. He was given some medication at the clinic but not the necessary antibiotics. The staff member who treated him, Nurse Richter, did not complete his clinic record accurately nor did she sign the said record. The prescription given was inappropriate to the symptoms the patient presented with. No proper observation, assessment examination or diagnosis took place.

Mr Teels' condition continued to deteriorate. Six days after visiting the clinic he went to another hospital, where he was admitted to the ICU with obstruction of the bowel.

Professional Nurse Richter failed to supervise the patient and to:
- appropriately observe, assess, examine and diagnose the patient's condition
- determine and maintain the patient's health status
- promptly refer the said patient to a medical practitioner when his condition clearly warranted such referral
- keep clear and accurate records of all actions performed in connection with the said patient.

Questions

1 In a ward situation the supervisor and supervisee interact. In a clinic setting a professional nurse treats and supervises a client on a one-on-one basis. Individual supervision has certain strengths and potential challenges. Read through the following strengths and challenges, and comment on them.

Strengths and potential challenges for supervision on a one-on-one basis

Strengths	Potential challenges
More time for client	Full weight of focus on individual client
Opportunity to create clearer and more focused objectives	Input from only one person (supervisor)
Highly personalised	Difficulties if supervisory relationship (nurse–patient) breaks down
Client can ask questions at own pace	Evaluation and feedback from one person's perspective only
Non-competitive environment	Can become collusive with little challenge
Allows client to concentrate on one particular issue	Can foster dependency in clients
Development in health can be easily monitored	Less comparison for clients about other ways of working
Supervisors' intentions can be geared specifically towards the patient	Transference issues may hamper health if unresolved

2 What type(s) of supervision was/were needed in this scenario?

Conclusion

Supervision is a process that requires reflective practice. As supervisors observe the thoughts and feelings of the patient or supervisee they are also aware of their own practice and how this can be influenced for the good by being with another. We also see ourselves through the eyes of others, which can lead to insight into our own behaviour.

Clinical/professional supervision is underpinned by a formal or unwritten agreement between the participants. In a clinic setting the professional nurse and patient have an agreement. This agreement or 'contract' makes explicit the nature and boundaries of the relationship. A session-specific agreement between participants can be negotiated at the beginning of each meeting or clinic visit, which will outline the goal(s) of that session and help clarify the steps needed to achieve them. Time within the sessions may be structured for helping to understand the pertinent issues and work towards a solution of greater understanding. The latter is also applicable in situations between a supervisor and supervisee.

Index

Please note: Page numbers in *italics* refer to figures and tables.